A Mother's Guide to
Raising Healthy Children—Naturally

A Mother's Guide to Raising Healthy Children—*Naturally*

SUE FREDERICK

Foreword by Jay Gordon, M.D.

KEATS PUBLISHING

LOS ANGELES

NTC/Contemporary Publishing Group

The purpose of this book is to educate. It is sold with the understanding that the publisher and author shall have neither liability nor responsibility for any injury caused or alleged to be caused directly or indirectly by the information contained in this book. While every effort has been made to ensure its accuracy, the book's contents should not be construed as medical advice. Each person's health needs are unique. To obtain recommendations appropriate to your particular situation, please consult a qualified health care provider.

Library of Congress Cataloging-in-Publication Data

Frederick, Sue.
    A mother's guide to raising healthy children—naturally / Sue Frederick.
       p. cm.
    Includes bibliographical references and index.
    ISBN 0-87983-926-0
    1. Pediatrics—Popular works. 2. Children—Diseases—Alternative treatment.
  3. Naturopathy—Popular works.

    RJ61.F915 1999
    649'.4—dc21   99-042973

Published by Keats Publishing
A division of NTC/Contemporary Publishing Group, Inc.
4255 West Touhy Avenue, Lincolnwood, Illinois 60646-1975 U.S.A.

Interior design: Freeborn Design
Cover design: Mary Lockwood
Cover photograph: © David J. Sams / Tony Stone Images

Printed in the United States of America

International Standard Book Number: 0-87983-926-0

99 00 01 02 03 04 VP 18 17 16 15 14 13 12 11 10 9 8 7 6 5 4 3 2 1

I dedicate this book to my daughter, Sarah.
For her wondrous spirit, light, and beauty, I am forever grateful.

Contents

Foreword by Jay Gordon, M.D., ix

Acknowledgments, xi

Introduction, xiii

Part 1   The Basics: Getting Off to a Healthy Start

1   The Benefits of Breast-feeding, 3

2   Nutrition: Feed Your Children Well, 11

3   Immunizations, 19

4   Nurturing and Loving Your Child: How to Create
      a Healthy, Happy Child, 31

5   Encouraging Your Child's Spiritual Development, 37

**Part 2   The Natural Approach to Common Childhood
             Illnesses**

6   A Stay-Healthy Plan for the Cold and Flu Season, 49

7   When Your Child Has a Fever, 55

8   Healthy Skin: Natural Personal Care for Kids, 61

9   Natural Remedies for Children's and Infants' Common
      Complaints, 67

Part 3   Complementary Therapies

10   Herbal Medicine, 115

11   Homeopathy: Safe and Simple Medicine, 125

12   Flower Essences: Helping Children Stay Healthy, 131

13   Chinese Medicine, 137

14   Nutritional Supplementation for Kids, 143

**Appendix A: A Child's Materia Medica: A Parent's Natural
                 Home Pharmacy, 153**

Appendix B: A Parent's Natural Home Health Kit, 195

Bibliography, 201

Index, 205

Foreword

I have been a pediatrician for twenty years and have looked at an estimated 500,000 ears during my medical career. Many times, the eardrums were inflamed or infected-looking. Because of my conventional medical training, residency, and postgraduate medical experience, I often have had to struggle to remember that every one of those ears was attached to a wonderful young child.

Sue Frederick's book has helped me—and would help every doctor, health-care practitioner, and parent—remember one crucial fact: A child's body will heal itself naturally if we stay out of the way and use gentle remedies, wisdom, and guidance.

I have seen the ability my thirteen-year-old daughter, Simone, has to heal herself, and I have watched thousands of other children do the same thing, often dealing with illnesses conventional (Western) treatment couldn't touch. I have also experienced tremendous frustrations when medical tools I acquired through my years of training fell short of alleviating pain and hastening healing.

We are all looking for ways to promote optimal health, strength, and well-being for our children and would like to do this nutritionally and naturally, without resorting to medications with potential side effects. *A Mother's Guide to Raising Healthy Children—Naturally* presents plans, details, and feelings in more accessible terms than I have ever seen them before. It is written from the perspective of a loving parent and aimed at other loving, intelligent parents. Sue Frederick's discussion of infant nutrition, vaccines, and infant sleep patterns should be required reading in medical school. The immune system, antibiotics, and disease prevention are covered in a manner that allowed even me—a doctor—to understand these crucial concepts in a natural light. Specific healing methods, elucidated with choices and concise methods of treating all the common childhood ailments could serve as a text for doctors, parents, and anyone else who takes care of children.

I am pleased and honored that Sue Frederick asked me to write this note at the beginning of her book. This is a superb, enlightening work which manages to entertain on every page.

—Jay Gordon, M.D.
Santa Monica, California

Acknowledgments

This book was the idea of Nathan Keats, the founder of Keats Publishing, who came to me with the title after having read one of my "Letters from the Editor" in *Delicious!* magazine. I'm grateful to Nathan for urging me to write a book even though I was the mother of a young child and working full-time as a magazine editor. I'm grateful to *Delicious!* magazine and its founder, Doug Greene, for launching my career in natural health journalism and encouraging me to find my voice and my audience in monthly letters from the editor. I'm thrilled to be editor of the Web site www.healthshop.com where, once again, I can reach thousands of people with a message of good health. I'll always be grateful to my friend Katherine Bergin, vice-president of healthshop.com, for her belief in my work and the career opportunities she has given me along the way.

It's truly a great blessing to bring a child into this world, and I have been very blessed to be the mother of my delightful Sarah. She is an inspiration in every way imaginable. Being her mom keeps me trying my best in all areas of life. And I deeply appreciate my own mother's generous spirit and strong encouragement. She taught me to love books from an early age.

A huge thank-you to the great friends and natural medicine experts who shared their knowledge, expertise, and experiences to help me write this book, especially Lara Pizzorno, a dear friend and excellent writer who wrote the natural remedies section, the materia medica, and the home health kit chapter. I have an enduring love for my first husband, Paul Frederick, who died of cancer in 1980. His love as well as the insights and wisdom he shared with me have molded my life and work every moment since his death. I remember my father every single day: He was, and always will be, my hero in every way, guiding me with love, kindness, and intelligence.

To my dear girlfriend, Crissie, I offer a great big hug and a warm thank-you.

There are no words to express my gratitude for my spiritual teacher, Swami Shambhavananda, and the great work he has shared with me.

Mostly I am grateful to you, the reader. Over the years, the feedback I've received from you, your sincere questions, and your loving support have assured me that this message of good health is indeed helpful.

Introduction

During my seven years as editor of *Delicious!* magazine and now as editor of healthshop.com, a Web site devoted to natural health information and products, I've heard from many new parents seeking advice about raising their children. Parents are faced with numerous health decisions, from immunizations to antibiotics, and sorting through all the books, magazines, and advice to find the best information can be an overwhelming experience.

As a new mother myself, I often turned to a number of experts during the first years of my daughter's life. In these pages I offer the information that is most helpful and practical, gleaned from my own experiences and from the opinions of top experts—the ones I trusted to help me in making my choices. I've put together this user-friendly guide because I understand your questions, concerns, and fears, and because I want to help you raise your baby in good health.

First, let's look at what conventional medicine has to offer you as a parent. Your pediatrician certainly will be helpful when your child is sick. Presumably, he will give you an accurate diagnosis; often an antibiotic will be prescribed as part of the treatment plan. Antibiotics are not the answer to every illness, however. Using antibiotics when your child has a minor ear infection, for example, can weaken the immune system, leaving the child more vulnerable to the next illness and to antibiotic-resistant bacteria. Your pediatrician probably will not explain how to boost your child's immunity to prevent future illness.

On the other hand, practitioners of natural medicine will teach you how to strengthen your child's immunity to disease through nutrition, herbs, and vitamins so that she either won't get sick at all or will recover more quickly with fewer complications.

Think of this book as a holistic health conference for your child. Imagine yourself sitting around a table with the most brilliant, insightful practitioners of complementary medicine today, from Jeffrey Bland, Ph.D., nutritional bio-chemist and chief executive officer of HealthComm International, a health education company in Gig Harbor, Washington, to health practitioner Janet Zand, N.D., L.Ac., O.M.D., author of *Smart Medicine for a Healthier Child*. Imagine being able to ask these experts how to keep your child as healthy as possible. You'll find their answers here. You won't hear them saying that antibiotics are the solution.

Natural medicine does hold the answers we're looking for. It offers a noninvasive, practical approach to preventing and treating disease using time-tested remedies such as herbs, vitamins, homeopathy, and a healthful diet. I've long been a believer in this system of health care, spurred in part by a traumatic experience in my thirties when my first husband died of colon cancer. Thus began my search for a different kind of medicine—one that *prevents* disease.

Many of us are fed up with expensive, risky, and ineffective conventional medicine and have taken charge of our health by consulting practitioners of natural medicine. During 1990, Americans made more visits to alternative practitioners than to primary care physicians, according to the *New England Journal of Medicine*. Furthermore, curing rather than preventing disease is costly, notes Joseph Pizzorno, N.D., president of Bastyr University in Seattle, Washington, and coauthor of the *Encyclopedia of Natural Medicine*: "Many physicians realize they've come to the limits of technologically oriented dis-ease intervention, and those limits aren't only scientific, they're financial. We can't afford the conventional medical system anymore. We need a new heal-ing paradigm, which promotes health rather than treats disease."

Fortunately, that new healing paradigm can be found in natural medicine, which focuses on prevention. It's clear that the cost of preventing disease is much less than the cost of treating disease, says Robert McCaleb, president of the Herb Research Foundation, a nonprofit educational organization in Boulder, Colorado. "Yet, the Food and Drug Administration has approved only three preventive medicines for over-the-counter use: fluoride tooth-paste, sunscreen, and motion sickness pills."

Natural practitioners such as McCaleb recommend several preventive remedies that are time-tested and have been proven effective in numerous European studies. "It's well documented that immune stimulants such as the herbs echinacea and astragalus defend against colds and flu," he explains, "while garlic, reishi mushrooms, and hawthorn berries help protect the cardiovascular system and lower blood pressure. And green tea extract, shiitake mushrooms, garlic, and antioxidants help protect against cancer."

McCaleb and other natural health proponents also find fault with modern medicine's approach to curing disease. "Most physicians know that the herb echinacea is more effective than antibiotics for treating bronchitis in children, and that antibiotics will interfere with recovery," he continues. "Yet they still prescribe antibiotics frequently, and we're all paying the price."

Since my husband's death twenty years ago, I've used primarily natural medicine to care for myself and my family. I'm more convinced than ever that preventing disease is the only path to good health, and the key to prevention lies in having a healthy immune system. We must find a way to raise our children to have strong immune systems—strengthened by breast-feeding and a nutritious diet, and not ravaged by the side effects of unnecessary vaccinations or weakened by antibiotics and poor diet. I believe children raised on low-sugar diets with few processed foods and abundant fresh, organic vegetables, who take vitamins and herbs instead of antibiotics, have a good chance of living a long, healthy life free from serious disease.

We have begun to clean up our planet, and now we must also clean up our health care. If we are to give our children the best possible chance to survive in this polluted world, it's imperative to begin making informed decisions, such as whether to breast-feed, even before a child is born. The choices you make now will inevitably impact on your child's future health.

PART 1

THE BASICS:
GETTING OFF TO
A HEALTHY START

Chapter 1

The Benefits of Breast-feeding

W hen I was born in 1951, my mother was not encouraged by her doctor to breast-feed me. In that era, breast-feeding was considered unnecessary and exhausting for the mother. Nowadays, the benefits of breast-feeding over formula-feeding are widely recognized, and most doctors encourage a new mother to breast-feed. Still, only 44.5 percent of America's mothers exclusively breast-feed in the hospital—quite a drop from 90 percent in 1920, but better than 21 percent in 1957.

New mothers need support and education when they start nursing their infants. It was a great relief to me when the hospital nurses did everything possible to help me get started breast-feeding after my daughter was born; they taught me to listen for the special gulping sound that signaled she was indeed getting my milk, and they allowed her to "room in" with me through the night.

Depending on the hospital in which your child is born, you may or may not receive the necessary lactation support. It's essential to prepare yourself ahead of time by reading books such as the La Leche League's *The Womanly Art of Breast-feeding,* which shows you how to avoid the pitfalls of nursing—such as sore nipples—and make the process a mutually satisfying one for mom and baby. It's also helpful to speak directly with someone from the La Leche League, a national organization dedicated to helping mothers breast-feed. They can be reached at 1–800-LALECHE.

IT'S YOUR CHOICE

When making your decision whether to breast-feed, please remember that it's your personal decision, and you should not feel guilty if you decide breast-feeding is not for you. Breast-feeding can be exhausting to the mother, and the baby often becomes more dependent on her. This doesn't work for some moms, especially if they must return to work right away.

If you do choose to breast-feed, there are other important considerations. Everything you eat and drink makes its way to the baby. That means no caffeine or alcohol, and whatever gives you gas will give the baby gas too. This can be frustrating, especially if you're craving that cup of coffee, glass of wine, or highly seasoned food.

Some mothers keep their babies in bed with them at night to facilitate nursing. I found that sleeping and breast-feeding went together quite well. Keeping my daughter in bed next to me was easiest for everyone. When she woke up crying, I simply rolled over, nursed her, and we both fell asleep again quickly. Other mothers are uncomfortable with this option. Whatever suits your family style, make sure that safety is your primary concern and that the infant is not at risk of falling out of bed or being rolled upon by an adult.

First, let's discuss the benefits of breast-feeding. Breast milk contains all the nutrients your newborn needs and is more easily digested and assimilated than any other infant food. Indeed, research has shown that mother's milk provides protective factors not found in any formula, actually inhibiting the growth of harmful bacteria and viruses in your baby's maturing body, and promoting the development of a healthy digestive system.

Every time your baby breast-feeds, she gets a healthy dose of antibodies to bolster her immunity to disease. As a result, she probably will get fewer colds, ear infections, and other illnesses than will bottle-fed babies. If a breast-fed baby becomes ill, recovery time may be quicker and with fewer complications. A recent study also suggests a decreased risk of childhood cancer in breast-fed babies, according to the authors of *What to Expect the First Year.*

There are great emotional advantages for both baby and mother during the nursing process. Your baby instinctively needs your smell, your closeness, your nurturing. The physical act of cradling a baby in your arms while you nurse fosters an emotional intimacy that is quite unique. You may be surprised by the depth of love and comfort you feel. I found it to be a very soothing experience for both my baby and me. Some women, however, find it difficult to relax while nursing. Breasts may be sore, tender, and engorged, making it painful when the baby clamps down on the nipple. Whenever I experienced this difficulty, I visualized angels wrapping us both in soothing light, sending love to my baby through my body. This visualization helped both of us relax, and my milk began to flow.

Kathryn Dewey, professor of nutrition at the University of California, Davis, has spent years researching the nutritional composition of breast milk and its effects on children's health. "Our studies have shown that even here in Davis, California, we have a significant difference in illness rates between non-breast-fed and breast-fed babies under two years old. Breast-fed babies just don't get sick as much as non-breast-fed babies," she explains.

Breast milk has a variety of antiviral and antibacterial components that protect against infection, reports Dewey. "The reduction in illness associated with breast-feeding is of sufficient magnitude to be of public health significance," she notes in her study, reported in the *Journal of Pediatrics*. Dewey compared growth, nutrient intake, illnesses, and activity levels during the first two years of life between infants who were either breast-fed or formula-fed until at least twelve months of age. She found that formula-fed infants were twice as likely to get severe diarrhea than breast-fed infants during the first year of life. She also found that formula-fed babies who attended day care were extremely susceptible to diarrhea, while breast-fed babies in day care were not.

In addition, prolonged ear infections lasting more than ten days were more frequent in formula-fed babies, and the percentage was 5 times higher in the first year of life and 3.6 times higher in the second year. Breast-fed babies are held in a semiupright position to feed, whereas bottle-feeding can be done while the baby is lying on his back. In this horizontal position, the liquid (formula or milk) easily flows into the child's eustachian tube where it can become blocked and create an ideal environment for bacterial growth. It is likely, explains Dewey, that although the feeding position of breast-fed versus bottle-fed infants and toddlers may explain part of this difference in ear infection rates, secretory IgA and prostaglandins in human milk reduce ear infections by affecting the ability of pathogens to cause an inflammatory response. Dewey notes that breast-feeding during the first year of life also reduces the incidence of diarrhea by 50 percent regardless of socioeconomic and educational levels of the parents.

Sandra Apgar Steffes, program coordinator for the UCLA Extension Lactation Training Program, which has been recognized by the U.S. Surgeon General as a model training program for the country, agrees with Dewey about the importance of breast-feeding. "I believe that all babies should be breast-fed. Human milk is superior to any other, and breast-feeding is easy," says Steffes. Her award-winning program has trained more than 4,000 health care professionals, including hospital-working R.N.s, M.D.s, registered dietitians, and La Leche League leaders to assist and educate breast-feeding mothers.

Steffes likes to remind women that the worldwide average age for children to be weaned from breast-feeding is 4.2 years old, and yet in our culture, nursing a four-year-old is considered abnormal. "I'm afraid that in this country the breast is most admired for its beauty, not its functionality," she notes. "It's such a great privilege to be a woman and be so close to the life force, to be able to sustain life with breast milk. Our bodies should be admired for their great functionality, more than their appearance."

THE PERFECT FORMULA

For the first few days after delivery, your breasts secrete a clear fluid called colostrum, an ideal first food for your baby, easily digested and abundant in antibodies, special proteins that defend the newborn against disease. These antibodies, known as immunoglobulins, are manufactured by the mother's immune system in response to infections and germs in her environment. One such protective factor is secretory IgA, which protects the baby at points most vulnerable to germ attacks, such as the throat, lungs, and intestines. The IgA in breast milk also stimulates the development of the infant's own immune system.

Colostrum contains more protein, electrolytes, minerals, salt, vitamin A, and nitrogen than mature mother's milk, but less fat and carbohydrate. It has nearly three times the amount of protein as mature milk because it has several amino acids and antibody-containing proteins not found in mature milk. It has higher levels of IgA and higher numbers of white blood cells.

Antibodies from colostrum have been found in the feces of breast-fed babies, but not in those who receive only formula, and researchers believe that the breast-fed baby's superior resistance to disease is due in part to these early antibodies.

Colostrum's main function is to protect newborns against infection, yet it also acts as a laxative to clean out the meconium from the baby's bowels. Meconium is the greenish-black waste matter formed in the baby's intestinal tract before birth.

Breast-feeding provides an immediate, on-demand supply of immuno-globulins specifically designed to protect your baby against viruses or bacteria that threaten his system. The nursing mother actually makes antibodies in response to microorganisms threatening her baby, even when the needed immunoglobulin isn't initially present in mom's blood. When a breast-fed infant is invaded by a new virus or bacteria, the offending germ is passed from baby to mother as baby nurses. Your breast actually produces the matching immunoglobulin and sends the protective element back to your baby through the milk.

Another important benefit is that breast milk contains generous amounts of essential fatty acids; specifically, an omega-3 fatty acid called docosa-hexaenoic acid, or DHA, which is lacking in cow's milk and formula. DHA is essential for optimal brain and nervous system development, and studies have shown that infant diets with reduced levels of omega-3 fatty acids can result in deficiency of DHA, which in turn may cause irreversible retinal damage.

Human milk also provides one and a half times as much lactose as cow's milk. When metabolized, lactose is broken down into two sugars essential to the maturing brain and spinal cord. Lactose also promotes the growth of friendly bacteria, *Lactobacillus bifidus,* in the baby's intestines. These bacteria aid digestion and protect the infant against undesirable bacteria that cause diarrhea.

During the first six months of a baby's life, a diet of breast milk alone helps prevent allergies, especially when the baby begins eating solid foods. The most common cause of food sensitivity or allergy during the first year of life is proteins such as those found in milk, eggs, cereals, or peanuts. While the protein in mother's milk is perfectly suited to her baby's immature digestive system, the proteins in formula, derived from cow's milk or soybeans, may not be. Cow's milk contains more than twenty-five proteins that can cause allergic reactions. For these reasons, researchers at the University of California, San Diego, recommend that the baby be six months of age before introducing foods other than breast milk.

Scientists agree that nursing is good for mom, too. As you breast-feed, the baby's sucking helps your uterus to contract and reduces the flow of blood caused by childbirth. Weight loss, particularly during the first three months postpartum, is greater in mothers who breast-feed than in those using formula. Breast-feeding mothers have a lower risk of conception, breast cancer, and osteoporosis, according to studies published in the *Journal of the American Dietetic Association*.

Sometimes, of course, it's impossible to breast-feed your baby. You may have adopted a child, you may have health problems, or the child may have health problems that prevent it. Once you start browsing the aisles of your local supermarket in search of a formula, however, you may be shocked at the ingredients.

When my daughter was an infant, I decided I needed a backup formula to keep on hand. My supply of frozen breast milk was dwindling, and she took bottles of expressed milk every afternoon while I was at work. I pumped breast milk as often as possible, but her appetite was increasing, and I couldn't keep up with her. After reading the labels and finding ingredients such as hydrogenated oils, I couldn't bring myself to buy formula.

I was fortunate to have an expert natural health practitioner to consult. Janet Zand, author of *Smart Medicine for a Healthier Child,* designed a goat's-milk-based formula specifically for Sarah. She added vitamin and mineral supplements and essential fatty acids based on Sarah's weight and health needs. It became my emergency formula to use whenever I ran out of pumped breast milk. Sarah tolerated it well, and it took some of the pressure off of me.

"The formulas on the market are not satisfactory," explains Zand. "Read the labels. There's no need to give a baby, who doesn't have a fully developed digestive system, hydrogenated oils. It's not an accident that almost every child who is put on formula initially develops digestive problems."

Zand cautions against designing your own formula without guidance. "It's very challenging to create a formula for an infant. It should be specific to the needs of the child. It's imperative to seek the guidance of a natural health practitioner."

If you're going to give your baby a store-bought formula, however, there are ways to improve it. "I recommend bifidus supplements [friendly bacteria] put right into the bottle," says Zand. "Also, just a drop of an essential fatty acid such as borage or flaxseed oil can make a big difference to your child. However, again, I encourage you to seek the advice of a natural practitioner for guidance."

Chapter 2

Nutrition
Feed Your Children Well

When my daughter, Sarah, was born, I wanted her, above all else, to be healthy. I had lofty ideas about never feeding her sugar or any type of unhealthy food. She would be raised on organic fruits and vegetables and whole grains.

As all parents know, however, when it comes to food choices, rigidity often creates more problems than it solves. I decided that my job was to educate rather than to harass. I learned to let her try foods I didn't approve of. I constantly reinforced her understanding that healthy food gives her energy so she can jump, run, play, and grow big and strong, and that sugary, unhealthy foods can make her sick. If we can educate our children, each day, about how their food choices affect how they feel, they eventually will make the right choices for themselves.

Jay Gordon, M.D., a pediatrician based in Santa Monica, California, and author of *Good Food Today, Great Kids Tomorrow,* believes we should start our babies off with healthy diets for the first few years of their lives but be flexible about birthday parties, Easter, Christmas, Hanukkah, and other special occasions. "There's a lot more of these occasions than I thought," notes Gordon. "But that's OK. It's still only a small percentage of the meals our kids eat. As children get to be four or five years old, they start to understand that there is a connection between the foods they eat and how fast they run, and whether their tummies hurt or not. At this age, they respond to pleasant explanations and will even try new food that is offered in a warm, loving atmosphere."

Dinnertime should not be a battleground, he explains. "Children learn to enjoy new, healthy foods at different paces. The more pressure and bribery we offer surrounding broccoli, the less likely kids are to eat and enjoy it."

Gordon disapproves of telling children, "If you eat your broccoli, you can have dessert." He says this is a very traditional and very flawed way to get kids to eat their vegetables. "Basically you're saying if you eat this food that you dislike, I'll reward you with food that you like." This approach sends the message that broccoli is undesirable, while dessert is desirable. "I suggest you offer whole foods, and then relax."

Think of yourself as an educator rather than an enforcer. You can help your child understand why some foods are better than others by giving a simple and clear explanation. Gordon calls a hamburger a "greaseburger" to paint a vivid picture in his child's mind.

Remember, what you keep on hand is what your family will eat. Paul Wenner, author of *Garden Cuisine* and creator of the GardenBurger, points out, "Anything you do in life requires a little planning to turn out well. Eating healthy meals simply requires advanced planning. When we're hungry, we go with what we've got on hand. So make sure that what you've got is both healthy and tasty."

WE ARE WHAT WE EAT

The food you feed your child creates the foundation for her future health. Although we must relax and educate rather than enforce, remember that vegetables and fruits provide abundant nutrients, vitamins, and minerals, which promote efficient digestion and elimination and may help protect against cancer and heart disease.

An important and often overlooked aspect of your child's diet is making sure that their water is filtered so that it is free from chemicals such as chlorine, and that their food is organic (raised without pesticides or herbicides).

Consider this: American farmers annually apply 700 million pounds of pesticides to their crops. Farmers in other countries use nearly twice as many pesticides on their crops as we do; we import many of these fruits and vegetables. Fresh fruits and vegetables get especially large doses of pesticides, with some being treated to a dozen or more applications per year, according to the National Research Council, an arm of the National Academy of Sciences. The Environmental Protection Agency (EPA) estimates that pesticides cause cancer in 6,000 Americans annually. Many members of the organic farming community believe this number is, in reality, much higher.

The potential impact of pesticide residues is more of a threat to children than to adults. Children eat far more fruits and drink more fruit juices relative to their body weight than do adults. Children's growing bodies, with their developing organs and tissues, are more sensitive and vulnerable to toxins than are the fully developed organs of an adult.

A report by Consumers Union (CU) found that Americans eat some fruits and vegetables that contain high enough levels of pesticide residues to cause concern. The study looked at twenty-seven foods, using data gleaned from U.S. Department of Agriculture tests of 27,000 samples from 1994 to 1997. Risk estimates were based on the number of samples containing pesticide residues and the amount of toxicity of each residue. The toxicity levels came from EPA data. CU combined the figures from the two federal agencies to compile a "toxicity index." Apples, grapes, green beans, raw peaches, pears, spinach, and winter squash were high on the risk scale. The highest amount of pesticides was measured in U.S.-grown peaches, which had ten times higher pesticide levels than peaches imported from Chile. The report concluded that even a single daily serving of some produce can deliver unsafe levels of toxic pesticide residues for young children.

Earl Mindell, Ph.D., author of *Parents' Nutrition Bible,* divides foods into three categories: the Good Guys (which includes whole grains, vegetables, and fruits); the Okay Guys (which includes natural sweeteners such as maple syrup); and the Bad Guys (which includes refined sugar, sugared breakfast cereals, candy, and carbonated soft drinks).

Go through your pantry and refrigerator and get rid of the bad guys. If you don't have any unhealthy foods in your house, you won't eat them. Then make a list of healthy snacks and post it on your refrigerator. When you're tired or in a hurry, consult the list and choose something. Remember, the contents of your refrigerator and pantry are like a classroom to your child. He will choose and experiment with foods that you provide. If tofu is never to be found in your refrigerator, your child won't try it. But if you make a tofu gardenburger for lunch and your child loves it, she will ask for it again.

A TYPICAL SNACK LIST

- Organic baby carrot sticks and dip
- Whole-grain crackers and low-fat cream cheese
- Organic broccoli florets and dip
- Organic apple slices and peanut butter
- Tofu burgers and tofu hot dogs
- Yogurt
- Fruit smoothies
- Nachos made with whole-grain corn chips and low-fat cheese
- Organic blueberries

Your eating habits send a strong message to your children. Seeing you fill up on potato chips does not encourage your child to eat carrot sticks. If you steam a head of cauliflower and enjoy it immensely, however, your child will be interested in trying it. (Maybe not now, but in the future.) Good dietary habits are formed during childhood. Children do what they see others doing. In the long run, they will choose what you choose.

SERVING MEAT:
A WARNING ABOUT *E. COLI*

Most experts agree it's best to base your child's meals on a plant-based diet. Dr. Gordon, the American Cancer Society, and Benjamin Spock, M.D., in his recent revision of *Baby and Child Care,* recommend raising children on a vegetarian meal plan. This doesn't mean you should never feed your child meat. If you base your meal plans around a main dish of meat night after night, your child will not get enough vegetables and whole grains. If you base your meals on rice, beans, whole grains such as quinoa, vegetables, and soy-based proteins such as tofu, he will receive all the nutrients he needs.

I can't emphasize enough how important it is to serve "clean" meat to your child. Superstrains of *E. coli* bacteria have been found in hamburgers (the most dangerous form of meat, since it is ground up and handled, allowing any contaminants to spread) and have caused numerous deaths. When meat is taken from an animal carcass, it is often contaminated with deadly

E. coli. In most cuts of meat, the bacteria remain on the top of the meat and are killed in the cooking process. In ground-up hamburger, however, the contamination can be spread throughout the meat and may be hidden in the very center. If the patty isn't thoroughly cooked to precise temperatures (at least 170 degrees), there is a chance that the burger will harbor *E. coli.*

Numerous bacterial pathogens such as *Salmonella* and *Listeria monocytogenes* can be found in all meats, but don't forget about the antibiotics, growth hormones, and a variety of pesticides and other man-made chemicals that can be passed from the animal to the meat to your child. Above all else, if you serve meat, make sure it is organic.

PACKING A HEALTHY SCHOOL LUNCH

A healthy school lunch? Sound improbable? It can be done! Keep it simple. Make tiny sandwich squares, accompanied by tiny rice cakes and hummus. Provide fresh fruit or vegetables such as baby carrots, apple slices, or blueberries. Ask your children to help you pack their lunch so that they can choose the healthy foods they'll eat.

I always offer my child several choices: Your lunch choice today is a tuna sandwich with carrot sticks, or hot noodles with string cheese and blueberries. She'll gladly choose one and help me make it. Pack cold cooked pasta in fun shapes such as corkscrews with a tasty dressing to dip them into. On cold days, a thermos of hot lentil soup or vegetable soup, along with some whole-grain crackers, makes for a healthy, nurturing lunch.

FAVORITE LUNCH-BOX FOODS

- Sliced organic turkey
- Vanilla yogurt with fresh blueberries
- Baby carrot sticks with dip
- Apple slices with peanut butter dip
- Whole-wheat crackers
- Tuna sandwich (cut into small squares)
- Organic low-fat popcorn
- String cheese

FRUIT JUICE AND
YOUR CHILD'S HEALTH

My daughter drank breast milk, water, Rice Dream, and goat's milk almost exclusively until she was about a year old. After that she continued to nurse but often asked for fruit juice. By the time she was three years old, she was drinking about 16 ounces of juice per day—especially in the summer. Colorado has a very dry climate, and she was always thirsty but rarely drank water. It was also her first year of preschool, and she was catching lots of viruses. I began researching the effects of fruit juice on children's health and discovered that the natural fruit juice she loved so well was making her more susceptible to viruses because of its high sugar content. Indeed, digestive problems, diarrhea, failure to thrive, chronic congestion, and lowered immunity top the list of health problems being blamed on the excessive sugar found in fruit juices, even "natural" juices.

"It takes eight apples to make an eight-ounce glass of pure apple juice, and that's a lot of sugar," reports Molly Linton, N.D., of Emerald City Naturopathic Clinic in Seattle, Washington. Children are drinking far too much fruit juice, she adds. "There's so much sugar in fruit juices, it's like giving your kids ice cream all day long."

In fact, it has become the norm to see toddlers and even infants drinking bottles of fruit juice instead of milk. The *Journal of the American College of Nutrition* reports that over 90 percent of all infants in the United States consume fruit juice by one year of age, and that children under the age of five drink approximately 5 to 7 ounces of fruit juice daily, with 11 percent drinking more than 12 ounces per day.

"From all the research on juice and children's health, it's clear to me that as a parent who often used fruit juice, I was naive about the question of how simple sugars in the diet impact digestive health," says Jeffrey Bland, Ph.D., an international authority on human biochemistry, nutrition, and health. "Many parents complain about diarrhea in their young children, or they complain that their children won't eat. These problems may be caused by excessive juice consumption, which causes the child to feel bad from gas and bloating. These symptoms severely diminish the appetite."

These digestive problems stem from the presence of sorbitol in juices, according to Bland. Sorbitol, a naturally occurring but nonabsorbable sugar alcohol present primarily in pear and apple juices and used extensively in "sugar-free" mass-market products, is not well absorbed and creates lower digestive disorders like diarrhea.

The American College of Nutrition concurs. At a recent conference on fruit juice consumption and children's health, researchers concluded that the amount of sorbitol, pectin, and fiber of each fruit juice determines its digestibility, and that some juices, such as white grape juice, which doesn't contain sorbitol, are better tolerated than others. The researchers also expressed concern that some juice drinkers might be substituting juice for more nutritious foods, while others might have problems digesting sugars such as sorbitol. "Both of these factors could adversely affect growth, contributing to the development of decreased weight and/or height," they concluded.

The major problem with fruit juice, however, is the sugar's effect on the immune system, reports Janet Zand, who has treated children at her clinic in Santa Monica, California, for twenty years. She sees numerous children with symptoms such as chronic sore throat or congestion, which she attributes to the sugars in fruit juices: "The excessive sugar in fruit juices, no matter which type of sweetener is used, causes susceptibility to yeast overgrowth—specifically *Candida albicans.* This can manifest as chronic nasal congestion, eczema, or throat and ear infections."

Linton also treats numerous children with this problem. "Children get too much sugar from juices. Any sugar reduces white blood cell count [an indicator of immune strength] for four hours. That's why kids get sick after Halloween or birthday parties. The viruses have a heyday after all that sugar consumption."

Wean your children from fruit juice by using a formula of one-third juice to two-thirds unsweetened herbal tea, suggests Linton. "Rose hips tea combined with white grape juice is delicious. You can slowly reduce the amount of grape juice until it's mostly tea."

Zand, the mother of a three-year-old, dilutes her son's fruit juice with water. "I've diluted it so much that now he doesn't even like fruit juice and prefers water. I carry water with me all the time. When he's thirsty, it's what I offer him, and he drinks it," she explains.

Just how much fruit juice per day is healthy for your child? The American College of Nutrition recommends less than 12 ounces per day.

NATURAL IS BETTER

Your natural foods retailer offers an array of 100 percent fruit juices such as white grape juice. The term *natural flavors* on the label usually indicates substances such as cassia, a natural oil from the flowers of the acacia faresiana tree used to give "body" to raspberry juice. Mass-market juice products using the term *natural flavors* often contain refined sugars, preservatives, and other chemically derived substances, yet under Food and Drug Administration definitions, they still qualify as natural flavors.

Another advantage of buying from a natural products store is that several juice manufacturers test for pesticides, sulfites, and other contaminants. Sulfite detection in grape juice is important. Although sulfites are listed as Generally Recognized As Safe (GRAS) in the U.S. Code of Federal Regulations, some people are sensitive to them.

Natural foods stores also sell numerous brands of organic juices, free of pesticides and other harmful chemicals. Children under the age of five should not ingest alar; organic foods protect a child from having to eat or drink something with that chemical in it.

When reading juice labels, note the sweetener used. If you find corn syrup, a popular sweetener in mass-market juices, consider looking instead for a juice sweetened with white grape juice. Corn syrup has little nutritional value, is high in fructose—naturally occurring but still a sugar—and can cause reactions in people with corn sensitivity. White grape juice is easier on the digestive tract, less refined, and provides vitamins A, C, and E, calcium, potassium, iron, and magnesium.

Jeffrey Bland advises, "Parents should pick 100 percent juice for their children with its natural balance of flavonoids, instead of giving them partial juices with flavorings and sugar added, which is the same as giving your child soda pop."

I was fortunate because my daughter understood why I didn't want her to drink so much juice and she cooperated. Together, we decided on white grape juice diluted 50 percent with water. Sometimes we combined chamomile tea and white grape juice. Eventually, her favorite blend became 30 percent white grape juice, 70 percent water, and a dropperful of ginger extract. It tasted like ginger ale and contained the added digestive benefits of ginger. It's easier than you think to limit your child's juice consumption, and the sooner you begin the switch, the healthier your child will be.

Chapter 3

Immunizations

After your baby is born, the pediatrician may give you a card listing a "schedule" for your baby's vaccinations. A brief look at this list reveals that your baby is due to receive thirty-four doses of ten different vaccines in his first years of life, starting with a hepatitis B vaccination when he's only twelve hours old.

If you grew up in the 1950s, you witnessed the polio epidemic sweep across America, to be stopped (apparently) by the Salk polio vaccine. If you haven't seen any news reports on the dangers of vaccinations, you may not be as concerned about immunizations as you should be.

However, if you're a parent of one of the estimated 140,000 children injured each year by vaccinations, you're already well aware of the dark side of immunizations. These include immediate reactions such as fevers, anaphylactic shock, convulsions, and even death, as well as the long-term permanent effects of epilepsy, paralysis, optic neuritis, Guillain-Barré syndrome, arthritis, deafness, encephalopathy, multiple learning disabilities caused by brain damage, and mental retardation. There is also evidence linking childhood vaccines to cancer, AIDS, and chronic illnesses such as multiple sclerosis and lupus.

"With vaccinations, we're suppressing the childhood diseases, but what is the trade-off in the long run?" asks Kathi Williams, director and cofounder of the National Vaccine Information Center in Vienna, Virginia. "Are we trading childhood diseases for chronic illnesses later in life? Why has there been a dramatic increase in learning disabilities, attention deficit disorder, autism, and autoimmune illnesses such as lupus and multiple sclerosis that coincided exactly with the introduction of mandatory vaccinations?"

Barbara Fisher, coauthor of *DPT: A Shot in the Dark* with Harris Coulter, a book on the dangers of the DPT (diptheria–pertussis–tetanus) shot, is concerned about the lack of longitudinal systemic studies examining the long-term effects of vaccines on children. Fisher and other parents involved with the National Vaccine Information Center helped pass the National Childhood Vaccine Injury Act of 1986, which awards money to families with children who are left permanently brain damaged or dead as a result of a vaccine reaction. By fall 1996, the federal vaccine injury compensation program had awarded over $700 million to more than 1,000 families.

Parents really don't understand that they are risking their children's health when they take them in for vaccinations, says Williams. Although the Food and Drug Administration (FDA) lists immediate reactions to vaccinations that include seizures, brain damage, and death, the long-term effects, such as learning disabilities and a damaged immune system, are harder to track yet may be the most dangerous of all.

"We really don't know how many children are injured by vaccinations each year because there's never been a large-scale study to find out," Williams continues. "In 1986, [the National Vaccine Information Center] helped pass legislation that made it mandatory for physicians to report vaccine injuries. The FDA is now receiving 14,000 reports of vaccination injuries per year. But the FDA estimates that this is only 10 percent of the actual injuries occurring."

Harris Coulter, Ph.D., author of *Vaccination, Social Violence, and Criminality,* believes vaccines cause brain injury that leads to allergies, autism, dyslexia, learning disabilities, and behavioral disorders. Vaccines damage the developing myelination process of the nervous system in children. This assault causes an allergic encephalitis (inflammation of the brain) with widespread effects. The developmental problems caused by vaccines occur in a large percentage of children. His theories are based on the dramatic increase in autism, minimal brain damage, and learning disorders since the introduction of vaccines.

"Parents need to get informed. It's another important health decision, like breast-feeding or natural childbirth, that parents need to make before their child is born," says Williams. "When their baby is only twelve hours old, he'll be given the hepatitis B shot unless the parents intervene. You need to have already done your research by then."

ONE PARENT'S STORY

In 1980, a mother who was unaware of the dangers of immunizations took her extremely bright and healthy two-and-a-half-year-old son for his fourth DPT shot. "He was so smart, already learning his numbers and letters. He played with a deck of cards and could name all of the numbers on the cards. He spoke in full sentences at two years old," remembers Barbara Fisher. Four hours after the vaccination, her son lapsed into convulsions and what's commonly called classic collapse shock reaction. "He slept without moving for six hours and didn't recognize me or know where he was." From then on, he was constantly sick, stopped eating, stopped growing, and wouldn't look at letters or numbers. Later he was diagnosed with brain inflammation causing neurological damage that resulted in numerous severe learning disabilities, including dyslexia. He has spent all of his school years in special institutions for the learning impaired.

Since then, Fisher has spent most of her time gathering information about the dangers of immunizations and trying to educate parents before they decide to immunize. She believes the health care and pharmaceutical industries have financial motives that "sacrifice a certain percentage of the population for the good of the community at large." She disagrees with physicians who argue that it's acceptable for a percentage of children receiving vaccinations to be injured in order to prevent widespread epidemics. "If your child is injured or killed by a vaccine, you and your family will live with that for the rest of your life. You must educate yourself about the risks."

Fisher believes the vaccine debate is at the center of the growing natural health care movement demanding that people take control of their own health care by educating themselves and making good choices. "We want to enhance the immune system, not destroy it. For the past fifty years we've used vaccinations as the cornerstone of preventive medicine, and coinciding with that is the advent of chronic illnesses, such as a 300 percent increase in epilepsy, asthma, learning disabilities, attention deficit disorder, and multiple sclerosis. These chronic, debilitating diseases are on the rise, and there are no scientific studies to see if multiple vaccinations in the early years of life—when the immune system is still being formed—could be a factor. We need a long-term clinical study on the effects of vaccinations on the human immune system."

Disease mutation is another concern. A person who contracts a natural form of a disease and survives it has permanent immunity. Yet Fisher says vaccines provide only temporary immunity: "Vaccine failure will become a major problem, as we've seen with measles. Measles has mutated into a more serious form of the illness. When babies are no longer protected by their mother's antibodies because their mothers have only been vaccinated and have no permanent antibodies to give them, infants are going to get a more severe form of measles. This is already happening. Because they didn't do the long-term scientific studies to begin with, the medical establishment didn't anticipate these problems."

THE VACCINATION INDUSTRY

Advocates in the growing movement to change our nation's immunization policy claim that the financial security of the drug companies is at the heart of the mandatory vaccine program in our country. Numerous disturbing facts have led to this accusation. Did you know that the booming vaccine industry (with estimated revenues of more than $1 billion a year in the United States alone) downplayed the fact that DPT shots caused brain damage at the rate of one case for every 62,000 fully immunized children? And did you know these shots kill at least two to four children a year and perhaps as many as 900 a year—including a number of misclassified SIDS (sudden infant death syndrome) victims, according to the National Vaccine Information Center?

Furthermore, a new, safer vaccine called the acellular DPT vaccine (DTaP), which is just now being offered to parents, has been available for decades and could have prevented numerous deaths and injuries. American pharmaceutical companies initially decided not to bring this safer vaccine to market because it would increase production costs and lower the drug's 50 percent profit margins, according to *Money* magazine.

Did you know that the only cause of polio in the United States for the past eighteen years has been the oral polio vaccine (OPV), which contains live poliovirus? There are no plans to take it off the market. Even people who were fully vaccinated against polio when they were children are susceptible to catching "contact polio" from recently vaccinated children. Why is this vaccine still given to 98 percent of the 20 million children who receive annual polio vaccinations in the United States? The inactivated polio vaccine (IPV), which is injected and is twice as costly to make, does not cause polio. Could there be a financial motive behind the pharmaceutical companies' insistence that the oral polio vaccine is still worth the risk? Yes, according to *Money* magazine.

Here's another frightening example: Even though the IPV does not cause polio, both it and the OPV are commonly made from monkey tissue, which contains viruses that are potentially harmful to humans. Yet a safer IPV using human tissue is available in Canada. The Canadian vaccine is, of course, more costly to produce.

"The pharmaceutical companies do a lot of research and development, spend lots of money, and need a market for their products. Well, here's a great market—mandatory vaccinations without any long-term clinical studies to examine the risks," says Williams.

The dangers of monkey viruses from vaccines are getting a lot of attention in laboratories across the country. Michele Carbone, Ph.D., a molecular pathologist at Chicago's Loyola University Medical Center, has linked the monkey viruses found in polio vaccines to human cancer. Indeed, other researchers such as Harvard medical professor Ronald Desrosier, Ph.D., and John Martin, Ph.D., a professor of pathology at the University of Southern California, are warning the government that monkey viruses can be dangerous to humans and may cause everything from cancer to AIDS.

In his research, Carbone has found that SV-40, a monkey virus, is a cancer-causing agent, and that this virus contaminated OPVs given to Americans in the 1950s. To make matters worse, Italian researchers reporting in the medical journal *Cancer Research* suggest that SV-40, originally introduced to humans through the OPV, is now being spread from mother to child in the womb. Researchers suggest it may be responsible for the 30 percent increase in brain tumors in the United States over the past twenty years.

The sharp increase in childhood allergies is being examined as well. Harris Coulter, Ph.D., expert on the pertussis vaccine and coauthor of *DPT: A Shot in the Dark,* believes vaccines and allergies are clearly connected. The more you vaccinate your children, he says, the more you increase their allergic state. "Vaccines play the role of hypersensitizing the individual, generally speaking, so that he or she becomes more allergic to such common foods as milk or peanut butter or wheat, which are highly allergenic substances to large numbers of the population."

There is also a suspected link between vaccinations and crib death, or SIDS. In 1975, a law was passed in Japan to prevent vaccination of children under the age of two. Shortly after that, crib deaths and infantile convulsions disappeared from that country. In 1988, the medical journal *Pediatrics* reported that when parents in Japan were later given the option to vaccinate children under the age of two, rates of crib death quadrupled.

The smallpox vaccine also has been linked to the AIDS epidemic. This finding is based on World Health Organization statistics revealing that the greatest spread of HIV occurred in places with the most intensive vaccination programs. AIDS appeared in African countries that had been inoculated against smallpox, while neighboring countries that did not receive the vaccine remained unaffected. The same was true in South America. The smallpox vaccine is a bovine virus derived from the pus inside a cow's udder. Researchers theorize that the bovine virus can create a dormant AIDS virus, which can become activated at some point.

PLAYING STATISTICAL ROULETTE

Proponents argue that some loss of life is acceptable in the wake of the benefits derived from vaccines. The International Association of Biological Standards sets the expected risk/benefit ratio that should allow vaccines to be used. According to the association, "The subject affected by an inoculation has, without doubt, made a special sacrifice in the interest of the general public."

In this statistical-roulette approach to health care, this is how the logic goes: It's OK if my two-year-old develops polio from the live polio vaccine and can never walk again. He has sacrificed his own well-being for that of the world at large.

As a mother, I find this logic particularly upsetting. I won't sacrifice my child's well-being for anyone. My maternal instincts tell me to protect her from danger at all costs. Fisher agrees: "I've had physicians tell me that I'm selfish because I won't subject my two younger, healthy children to vaccines. They say I'm putting the community at risk. However, they want to put my children at risk of brain damage and death from immunizations, and that's OK with them. It's not with me."

Proponents also say that vaccines are responsible for the decline of polio and smallpox. Researchers know that infectious diseases were already in decline before vaccines were introduced. After World War II, the incidence of infectious disease started dropping on its own due to clean water, central heating, and a higher-quality food supply.

Indeed, there is some evidence that vaccines even increase death rates from the diseases they inoculate against. In the fifteen years following the introduction of the diphtheria vaccine in 1894, the number of diphtheria deaths in England and Wales rose 20 percent. Between 1895 and 1907, there were 63,249 cases of diphtheria in vaccinated individuals; 8,917 people died, a fatality rate of 14 percent. In the same time period, 11,716 cases were not treated with vaccines; only 703 died, a fatality rate of 6 percent.

In 1926, the American Medical Association started a drive to abolish diphtheria by 1930. Despite these efforts, states giving the largest number of diphtheria vaccinations in turn had the highest diphtheria death rates by 1930. For example, Michigan had one of the highest rates of inoculation and the highest rate of diphtheria deaths. In England from 1871 to 1880, during a period of compulsory smallpox vaccination, the death rate from smallpox leaped from 28 to 46 per 100,000.

REACTIONS TO VACCINATIONS: THE HARD FACTS

Polio

Given at two, four, and six months of age with boosters between four and six years old, this vaccine is designed to protect against poliomyelitis. Since 1979, the only cases of polio reported in the United States have been caused by the live OPV.

In 1994, the Institute of Medicine found compelling scientific evidence that the live OPV can cause paralytic and nonparalytic polio that can end in death. The Centers for Disease Control estimated that the risk is one case of vaccine-associated polio per 520,000 first OPV doses administered to an individual, and one case per 12.3 million for subsequent doses. The Institute of Medicine also concluded that the OPV can lead to poliovirus infection and death in individuals who come in close contact with those who have been recently vaccinated with OPV. The institute also determined that the OPV can cause Guillain-Barré syndrome, including death, and that the risk is approximately 2.5 per 100,000 people. Guillain-Barré syndrome is a rapidly progressing form of polyneuropathy characterized by muscle weakness, numbness, pain, and paralysis. Symptoms may not appear until four weeks following vaccination.

Both the OPV and IPV (which may not cause live polio) are made from monkey tissues that have been scientifically proven to carry viruses. Scientists have linked these viruses to AIDS, cancer, and other immune and neurological dysfunctions such as chronic fatigue syndrome.

DPT

The diphtheria-pertussis-tetanus (DPT) vaccine, given at two, four, six, and eighteen months with a booster between four and six years old, has been associated with more severe reactions than any other vaccine. The most frequently reported reactions include prolonged crying for more than three hours, high-pitched screaming, collapse/shock, fever over 103 degrees, excessive sleepiness, and convulsions. Some researchers believe that if your child experiences any of these symptoms, they have sustained brain injury that may range from mild (as in learning disabilities) to serious (as in mental retardation).

The British National Childhood Encephalopathy Study, the largest and most highly controlled study of brain damage in children ever conducted, found that one in 110,000 DPT shots results in brain inflammation, and one in 310,000 results in permanent brain damage.

According to the scientific literature on infant deaths following vaccine reactions, the DPT vaccine can cause infant deaths that are sometimes misclassified as SIDS.

The acellular version of the vaccine, DTaP, was licensed for use in infants in 1996. This version is considerably safer; however, most of the mild and serious reactions following DPT vaccination also have been reported following DTaP. It is believed, though, that DTaP produces reactions in a smaller number of children.

According to Kathi Williams, even with the advent of DTaP, there are still reports of seizures in children following the vaccination. "As the FDA puts it, there is no vaccine that's 100 percent safe and effective. The toxins in pertussis bacterium are very dangerous, and they're still included in the acellular version in order to make it effective. However, there will always be reactions to those toxins in the vaccine," she says.

Tetanus

In 1994, the Institute of Medicine concluded that tetanus and diphtheria-tetanus vaccines can cause Guillain-Barré syndrome including death, and death from anaphylactic shock. Too few studies have been done separating out the tetanus component to determine whether tetanus alone or with the diphtheria vaccine can cause other serious health problems reported with the DPT vaccine. Reported reactions from tetanus and diphtheria-tetanus have included residual seizure disorder, demyelinating diseases of the central nervous system, peripheral mononeuropathy, arthritis, and erythema multiforme (lesions of the skin or mucous membranes).

HIB

The *Haemophilus* influenza type B (Hib) vaccine, administered at two, four, six, and twelve months, is given to prevent bacterial meningitis, a potentially life-threatening disease with possible long-term side effects such as hearing loss and learning disabilities. It's required before a child can enter preschool. However, serious vaccine-associated reactions have been reported, such as convulsions; anaphylactic allergic reactions; serum sickness–like reactions such as joint pain, rashes, and edema; and occasionally death within four hours of vaccination. In addition, several cases of proven Hib invasive disease (meningitis) have occurred soon after immunization.

Hepatitis B

The hepatitis B vaccine, now given twelve hours after birth, with boosters at one and six months, has numerous side effects linked to its use. In 1994, the Institute of Medicine reported that there is compelling scientific evidence that the hepatitis B vaccine causes anaphylactic shock. In 1990, the *Journal of Pediatric Child Health* mentions pertussis as a side effect, as well as six serious illnesses in a series of 200,000 hepatitis vaccinations—including multiforme, aseptic meningitis, and grand mal seizure. The vaccine was also responsible for fifty-six minor illnesses, among them neurological tremors, Bell's palsy, hives, herpes zoster, joint inflammation, hepatitis-like illness, influenza-like syndrome, diarrhea, vomiting, and headache. The study's authors concluded that until further evidence could be gathered on possible side effects from the hepatitis B vaccine, it may be worth only "giving the vaccine to people at high risk, rather than to all the population."

Measles, Mumps, Rubella

The measles, mumps, rubella (MMR) vaccine is administered when the child is fifteen months old. Measles, mumps, and rubella are fairly innocuous childhood diseases. Good nutrition, clean sanitation, and proper medical care can prevent the side effects and complications such as hepatitis, convulsions, and meningitis that doctors always mention as a reason to choose the vaccine. Measles is indeed dangerous in Third World countries or in underprivileged communities with poor living conditions, sanitation, nutrition, and substandard health care. Vaccine-acquired immunity is questionable. In clinical studies, vaccinated children have been shown to contract these diseases when exposed to them.

In the past, some researchers believed that having measles as a child helped the human immune system to mature, priming it to be more effective when dealing with challenges from viruses and bacteria later in life. Recovery from natural measles infection confers lifelong immunity, while vaccine-induced antibodies provide temporary immunity. In fact, the majority of severe complications arise when contraction of the disease occurs in vaccinated individuals. In adults, these diseases pose an elevated risk of complications and debilitating side effects.

In addition, reactions that occurred immediately after the administration of a vaccine included encephalopathies (brain damage), aseptic meningitis, cranial nerve palsy, learning disabilities, and mental retardation.

Chickenpox (Varicella Zoster)

Reactions to the chickenpox vaccine, given at twelve months of age, include lesions on the body within four weeks of vaccination and fever of 102 degrees, upper respiratory infection, fatigue, disturbed sleep, diarrhea, vomiting, otitis media (ear infection), headache, hives, and febrile seizures. Because it contains live chickenpox virus, vaccine makers warn that vaccinated individuals potentially may be capable of transmitting the virus through close contact. Therefore, close contact with high-risk individuals such as newborns and pregnant women should be avoided after inoculation.

The death rate for chicken pox is 1.4 per 100,000 cases in healthy children but rises to nearly 31 per 100,000 cases in adults. There is some medical concern that mass vaccination with chickenpox vaccine will drive the disease out of the normal childhood population, where it is mild for most children, and into the infant and adult populations, where it can be more dangerous. Vaccine makers state that the duration of protection is unknown at present, and the need for booster doses is not defined. This questionable rate of efficacy may contribute to cases occurring in older age groups in the future.

There is also concern that injecting children with a live varicella zoster vaccine may cause the virus to lay dormant in the body and be reactivated later in life in the form of herpes zoster (shingles).

YOUR RIGHT TO CHOOSE

"We need to get information to the public about the side effects of vaccines so people can make informed decisions," explains Fisher.

Williams concurs: "It's very important that parents cut through what they're being told to do by their physicians and do their own research. I see a real trend in parents selecting certain vaccinations based on the needs of their child. For example, if you live in the country, you might want to give your child the tetanus vaccine. If you're a mom with hepatitis B, you may want to vaccinate your child against it. However, not all vaccines are appropriate for all children."

Even if you choose to vaccinate your child, you may spread out the immunizations so that your child doesn't receive more than one or two vaccines at a time, and you can begin vaccinations when your child is older. Some researchers believe the quantity of vaccine given at any one time is partly responsible for reactions. There is some evidence that giving vaccines to infants is more dangerous than giving them to children over the age of two.

If you choose not to vaccinate, find out what the vaccination laws are in your state. Religious, medical, and philosophical exemptions are worded differently from state to state. Ask your local librarian to help you obtain a copy of the law, along with any public health codes or education and welfare laws pertaining to vaccination requirements for school enrollment. All fifty states allow medical exemption to vaccination in the form of a signed statement by a medical doctor.

This is the avenue I chose for my daughter. Although my pediatrician didn't agree with my choices, he was well aware of the controversy surrounding vaccination and, after discussing it with me, was willing to sign a statement exempting her.

The National Vaccine Information Center has compiled an information sheet telling parents to ask themselves eight important questions before vaccinating their children.

1. Is my child sick right now?
2. Has my child had a bad reaction to a vaccination before?
3. Does my child have a personal or family history of vaccine reactions, convulsions or neurological disorders, severe allergies, immune system disorders?
4. Do I know if my child is at high risk of reacting?
5. Do I have full information on the vaccine's side effects?
6. Do I know how to identify a vaccine reaction?
7. Do I know how to report a vaccine reaction?
8. Do I know the vaccine manufacturer's name and lot number? Call 1-800-909-SHOT for information (Web site: www.909shot.com).

Do as much research as possible so that you can make an informed decision about this controversial topic. I hope this chapter has helped you know which questions to start asking. And I hope that in the future, mothers won't be faced with such difficult health care dilemmas.

Chapter 4

Nurturing and Loving Your Child

How to Create a Healthy, Happy Child

Perhaps the most important aspect of raising a healthy child is to provide emotional nurturing. If your child feels truly loved and knows that you'll always be there for her, that inner peace and sense of security will help strengthen her immunity and ability to fight off illnesses. Many researchers, such as Aletha Solter, Ph.D., agree with this theory. Solter, a developmental psychologist and mother of two, published a controversial book entitled *The Aware Baby*. In her books and workshops, Solter bravely proposed that babies, children, and even adults need to cry—have, in fact, a biological need to cry—in order to heal past traumas (such as birth trauma) or remembered pains. These remembered pains can be as simple as when an infant watches Mom walk out of a room and fears she'll never return. Solter also proposed that children's cries always need to be answered with loving attention—never ignored.

CRYING IS THE SOLUTION, NOT THE PROBLEM

In the first few years of life, babies form lasting opinions about themselves, other people, and the world around them. If a baby's cries are unanswered, he comes to believe the world is unpredictable, and that he can't trust other people. The baby learns that he is powerless and helpless to get his needs met and feels unlovable and unimportant. Solter feels that the parent who responds each time a child cries creates the opportunity for the child to learn trust and empowerment and to know that she can affect the environment through her actions.

In our society, crying is considered the problem rather than the cure. "Babies and children are told 'You'll feel better if you stop crying.' Just the opposite is true," explains Solter. "Crying is the process of becoming unhurt, and children will not feel better until they have been allowed the freedom of tears."

Clinical research shows that when an infant or young child is held lovingly and encouraged to cry instead of being hushed, left alone, nursed, or given a pacifier or bottle (unless they're truly hungry), the child will cry out, or "discharge," negative feelings such as pain, fear, and anger and become an emotionally healthy, happy child. It's essential to determine first that all of the baby's physical needs have been met, and that the child is not hungry, cold, wet, in need of a diaper change, or in physical pain. If the child continues to cry after the above needs are met, assume that a "discharge" is needed.

Hold the child lovingly and allow it to cry, even if the tears last as long as an hour. The baby will be renewed, refreshed, and delightful to be around, usually for the rest of the day. A child who is allowed to do this daily will be able to continuously heal inner pains, fears, and traumas as she grows, and become a truly healthy adult and functional member of society.

Research by William Frey, Ph.D., a biochemist at the St. Paul–Ramsey Medical Center in Minnesota, shows a biochemical reason for crying. Frey suggests the purpose of crying is to remove waste products or toxic substances from the body through tears. He has identified substances in tears, specifically the hormone ACTH and the catecholamines epinephrine and norepinephrine, which accumulate in the body as a result of stress. These substances are eliminated from the body along with manganese, an element that can have toxic effects on the nervous system if there is too much of it in the body.

We can help our children, notes Solter, by listening to them attentively when they cry. Reflect their emotions back to them with comments like: "Go ahead and cry. You're really angry right now. Just get all those angries out." This approach is healthier for your child, she explains, than trying to stop the crying by distractions or punishment.

Obviously, it's impossible to prevent a child from experiencing stress and pain in life. However, children who are permitted to express themselves have a better chance at successfully negotiating life's traumas and being emotionally healthy.

Solter stresses the importance of sleeping with young children from birth to age four or five (human beings are the only species that leave their young alone in the dark at night—a terrifying experience for infants). Her theory is based on the instinctual need of humans to be protected in order to survive. Sleeping with your child is not a popular idea. Parents tend to leave children alone in their rooms to cry until they become used to sleeping alone. The rationale is that the baby will cry about thirty minutes the first night, ten minutes the second night, and by the third night he'll be "cured" and fall asleep without crying.

This method works for the parents but is harmful to the child. Solter believes it diminishes the baby's trust in the parents, fosters a feeling of helplessness in the child, and leads to childhood fear and anxieties that can last a lifetime. Instead, she recommends holding the baby and paying attention to her while she cries: "She will then have an opportunity to cry, and when she has finished crying she'll fall into a peaceful sleep and won't awaken when you put her down."

Stopping your baby's cries with a pacifier, bottle, or nursing has many long-term ill effects, according to Solter, who calls them control patterns. These accumulated tensions prevent a child from growing, developing, and learning in a healthy way, and they lay the groundwork for emotional problems later in life. Solter also believes these control patterns become addictions, as the child goes from one substance that quiets her troublesome feelings (such as nursing or baby formula) to another substance such as sweets or alcohol.

Many parents believe punishment is a necessary tool for teaching correct behavior. Solter disagrees. She cites numerous studies to show the detrimental effects of punishment: children quit exploring and learning about their world because they fear the consequences of a wrong action; they become aggressive toward other children because they've been treated aggressively; and they learn to lie and deceive adults so they won't be punished again.

Learning to Listen

Solter advocates building a listening relationship with your child from the start to foster unconditional acceptance. When a child cries or "rages," the process is a healing one.

Linda Quigley, a social worker and director of the Family Nurturing Center in Boulder, Colorado, as well as a nationally certified trainer in the Nurturing Parenting program, agrees with Solter. Since 1975, in Quigley's work with disturbed children, she has seen numerous examples of the healing power of expressing and releasing troublesome feelings. Adults are trained from early childhood to repress emotions, and they become conflicted about how to handle emotions: "It's not the feelings we have that get us in trouble, it's the ones we didn't get to have since the day we were born that cause the problems."

Quigley incorporates the three techniques of mirroring feelings, listening attentively, and joining in with the person in pain, in combination with encouraging crying to assist even the most severely disturbed children.

In working with one clinically depressed little boy who had been badly abused, she experienced the power of simply reflecting feelings. The child was isolated in his world of pain and wouldn't communicate. Quigley sat beside him and tried to align herself with his physical posture, which expressed his pain, and with his slow breathing. "As he took a big sigh, I sighed too and said gently, 'That's right, you're really so, so sad.' After a while, he completely opened up to me, and a lot of healing took place," she remembers.

Quigley believes we are always communicating with each other, even when no words are exchanged, and that remembering this will help us interact with children more effectively.

It's important to understand that while every emotion is OK, every behavior is not. If a child is acting aggressively against other children or pets, it must be made clear that those actions are not acceptable, even though the emotions are.

The Link Between Emotional and Physical Health

Emotional health and physical health are deeply intertwined. A person who is depressed, for example, has lowered immunity to disease. Cortisol, a hormone that we produce while under emotional stress, is responsible for this because it interferes with healthy bodily functions including immunity. Researchers have found that crying reduces cortisol levels in the body—thus allowing immunity to improve.

We must supplement the medical care of sick children with emotional support in order to help them heal. "When kids are sick with a high fever, they don't cry because it takes too much energy. When they start to get better, they'll do more crying, and that crying is important for healing. Hold them and allow them to cry," suggests Solter.

When people pay attention to their physical pain and truly experience it, the pain goes away faster than if they try to ignore it. The same is true of emotional pain. Children understand this instinctively.

Until I began working on this book, I had rarely allowed my daughter, Sarah, to cry. She had nursed "on demand" as an infant and always received immediate comfort from the breast. However, she had numerous fussy days as an infant and numerous temper tantrums as a toddler. Solter says that I used nursing as a control pattern, even though that was not my intent.

As I've changed my approach to Sarah's crying, I've seen a remarkable shift in her behavior. When she gets upset about something now, I hold her in my arms (even if she struggles to get away from me) and whisper to her lovingly, "Go ahead and cry it out, baby. You're really angry and you'll feel better when you cry it all out." She'll often scream and cry for ten minutes, then she's done and usually is calm and happy.

HEALING OUR OWN PAIN

It's a glorious revelation when you realize that motherhood provides you with an astounding opportunity to heal your own past traumas. I have found this to be quite true for me. As I've held and loved Sarah through her infancy and childhood, I've been able to heal many of my own wounds from childhood. In 1951, the year I was born, my mother wanted to be a good mother and listened to everything her misguided physician told her to do: don't nurse your baby, put her on a strict feeding schedule, and don't hold her too much or you'll "spoil" her.

Solter claims that children who aren't held enough as babies spend much of their adult life seeking physical contact, often in inappropriate ways. Being a mom offers an opportunity to heal that unresolved pain.

Many mothers are forced to miss this tremendous healing opportunity because they must return to work soon after the birth of their child. Solter doesn't criticize working mothers, but she says these women should realize that both child and mom will reap great long-term emotional benefits if they can spend as much nuturing time together as possible.

I urge you to read Solter's books on child rearing. Even if you don't agree with everything she says, I believe you'll find parts of her theory that will improve your mothering skills, as they did mine.

Chapter 5

Encouraging Your Child's Spiritual Development

A s I sat down to write this section, the airwaves were filled with the painful news of the 1999 shooting at Columbine High School in Littleton, Colorado, in which fifteen students were killed.

This was a tragic and deeply disturbing event, and every parent's nightmare. As a mother, I felt the terrible grief of those parents who sent their children off to school in the morning and never saw them alive again. Yet I am also disturbed by the debate among the experts as to the reasons for the violence in our schools.

What could cause two young boys to resort to such anger and violence? Some experts say it's because of the easy access to weapons in our culture. Some say it's because there is too much violence in our television, movies, and video games. I believe we have lost our connections to one another and to God. Our communities have broken down. Children often grow up without any sense of connection to adults other than their parents. And if that bond is itself weak, the children are basically set astray with no one to turn to for help. If our children don't grow up with a strong sense of higher purpose, a strong connection to people and to God, they are easy prey for the darkness of our world. As parents, it is our job to connect them, first to ourselves, then to God and the community.

One's spirituality is a personal matter, and there are many paths to God. Regardless of the path you take, God must be a part of your child's life.

Many parents today say they don't want to indoctrinate their children into a particular religion or form of spirituality. I disagree. Our culture indoctrinates children to focus on material possessions and to doubt the existence of anything beyond what they can see. The early years provide an opening for a child's natural spirituality to blossom. Their belief in God is so honest that it has helped many a parent reconnect with God. It is essential to nurture the awareness that we are sacred and that God exists; if you never believed as a child, it's a long, difficult road to finding God when you're older.

Share your beliefs with your child about why we are here and who we really are. If you don't believe in God, discuss that as well. Open the doors for their own explorations into spirit. You may learn something from them. Children are very much in touch with the divine. They can heal your spiritual pain by sharing their insights with you.

There are many ways of inspiring and fostering the divine in children. Here are the thoughts of a diverse group of people who have been successful in doing just that.

JEFFREY BLAND, Ph.D., nutritional biochemist, CEO of Health-Comm International, Gig Harbor, Washington. Now that my "children" are thirty, twenty-seven, and seventeen, from what they have told me, the biggest contribution they received in spiritual training as children was the time we shared, starting at about age seven for each of the boys, hiking together in wilderness areas. They have all commented that these experiences and the many discussions we had at night on the trail deeply imprinted a feeling of sacredness, spirituality, and a sense of something bigger than they were. I think my takeaway is: have experiences in nature with your child and celebrate the beauty of the world in which we live and the spirit we feel as part of it.

LARA PIZZORNO, master's in divinity, researcher, health writer, and mother of one son. This is such a personal area, I'd guess loving parents have many different viewpoints about it. As Christ said, "My father's house has many mansions." Anyway, here's my take on it. Spirituality is perhaps the most individual and unique aspect of each of us. A child's spirituality is, in many senses, closer to a real understanding of the Absolute than an adult's, which has been layered over with the accretions of socialization, organized religion, and history, both personal and cultural. As Wordsworth put it in the poem "Intimations of Immortality," "Not in utter nakedness do we come from God who is our home, but trailing clouds of glory." For me, the first rule of the spiritual relationship I share with my son is to respect and value his spirit. His spiritual insights are often purer and more transcendent than mine are. He is not locked into what is, but is still able to freely envision what could be. It is my belief that fortunately, for the human race, our children are not little spiritual replicas of their parents, but fully fledged, autonomous beings. So what can a parent do to help nurture and protect a child's closeness to God? The exact actions depend upon what the parent is able to give and what the child is willing to receive. What I try to do is live my principles, integrate my faith into my daily actions, pray, be thankful for the many gifts with which we are showered every day—the beauty of nature, the love of my family, work I value, the fun of sharing our lives with pets, the joy of playing the piano or learning new things—and to share this with my son. When I make choices of any consequence, they are always based on a spiritual foundation, and I try to explain how it is operative in my choice to my son. When I feel wonder or thankfulness or joy, I pray— usually a silent prayer of thanks, but I share the fact that I am praying and why with my son. I try to go to church services at least every other week, and Galen often comes with me. When we are faced with difficulties or sadness, I try to think it through using my faith, and I try to share my thought process with my son. I also listen to his. And I try to answer his questions about spirit, life's meaning, God, to the best of my ability. I always preface anything I say with "This has been my experience," or "In my life, this has been proven true to me." And I always tell him he needs to test my insights and beliefs against his, keep what he finds to be true, and trust his own spirit and relationship with God—that his understanding will deepen and expand as his life experiences and challenges provide him with the lessons he needs to learn. Finally, when I tuck him in at night, I always tell him to rest well and be at peace, that God loves him and so do I.

JANET ZAND, L.Ac., O.M.D, N.D., author of *Smart Medicine for a Healthier Child*. My husband and I have two sons, Aubrey, who is on his way to college next year, and Michael, who is five. When Aubrey was very young, both his mother and father were staunch atheists. I met my stepson Aubrey when he was seven, and I was pleasantly surprised to learn that despite his parents' beliefs, he had developed into a young Taoist. At eighteen years old, he reads books about Eastern religion and through discussion with family has developed his own belief system with all the sophistication and subtlety of a person much older than his years. Like many five-year-old children, Michael has a passionate interest in God. He asks where God is, what He looks like, does He have friends, if you go to heaven will He be there, who else will you see, will there be angels, will he himself become an angel, is it a good idea to die so you can become a flying angel? Given that we have never formally discussed any of these concepts, it fascinates me that he has a grasp of this. I can only assume from all of this that children have innate spirituality. Perhaps it is the recentness of their experience with the Divine, their birth, I don't know. What is clear to me is that children do not need to be indoctrinated or coerced into spirituality. They naturally know it, feel it, live it. Generally, children simply need to be nurtured in the direction that they are already taking. As adults we can learn a lot about spirituality by witnessing our children.

ELIZABETH BERTANI, writer and consultant in the natural products industry for more than ten years. I raised my children to have a sense of spirituality and connection to God and the universe without belonging to a formal religion or following a guru or teacher. When my children were very young, we said the "Now I lay me down to sleep" prayer each night, and I talked to them about the protection of angels. Mostly we talked about the many ways one communicates with God, and that spirituality was based on the basic virtues of kindness, tolerance, and generosity. I tried to show by example that how one lives one's life is more important than a specific form. Each was free to choose a religious or spiritual practice, if so inclined. Experiencing each of my children as wonderful, caring adults and now as parents has assured me that each has a powerful sense of spirituality. I'm very pleased with their unique paths.

JACKIE ROOS, Florida public school teacher, Transcendental Meditation teacher, and mother of one. Basically, we feel we have nurtured Gillian's spirituality by first and foremost trying to be good examples to her. Children must see by their parents' behavior that they are actually living the universal principles of all the great religions: compassion, generosity, non-violence in speech and action. Secondly, we believe meditation is the keystone of a spiritual life, and from the time she has been a toddler, she has seen us meditating consistently morning and evening. Other than this, the three of us have had many conversations about God and ways to live a spiritual life in the midst of this complicated world. Finally, we have exposed her to Hinduism, Buddhism, and Christianity. We have built what we hope is a firm foundation, and from this, when she is ready, we think she will choose a path that feels right for her.

HEIDI DORFMEISTER, Montessori preschool teacher for more than twenty-five years and founder/owner of a Minnesota Montessori school. My son Jake [nine] is very spiritual: he likes to pray, talk about God, read Bible stories. Mitch [twelve] is somewhat agnostic. He talks about God when he needs something. I have a couple of theories. One is that Mitch identifies with David, my husband, who is cynical toward religion. Jake identifies with me. Jake has a personality that is introspective and deeply sensitive. Mitch questions everything and rejects most everything. I think a child's spirituality comes from the parents' guidance. Jake shows a sensitivity and interest in things spiritual, so we talk more about it. I think you have to set an example of being a "good" person in words and deeds, deeds being the most important. It is definitely something that needs to be addressed. We seem to be having a spiritual crisis going on.

LAXMI (FAITH STONE), meditation teacher at Shoshoni Yoga Retreat in Rollinsville, Colorado, wife of Swami Shambhavananda, and mother of a six-year-old. Living spiritually is, to me, not about following abstract esoteric ideals but about having practical forms of living love in your life. Two of my favorite verses are "God is Love" from the Bible and "Kindness is my religion" from the Dalai Lama of Tibet.

If I were to summarize the little things I do to encourage spirituality in my daughter, it would include the following items:

1. *Live it yourself.* A woman saint from India, Shree Maa, often tells children, "The mother is the first Guru, then the father." Parents are so very important to a young child. When young children see their parents practicing devotion, meditation, chanting, and mantra, and

when they sense love and devotion for God in the parents, the love in
their own hearts is easily kindled. Young children are so much closer to
purity, love, and devotion. It seems to come naturally for them. At our
ashram, we have the children help with the *arati* [singing and dancing
in devotion to the gods]. The joy, simplicity, and sweetness in their *arati*
is very moving for everyone. Sometimes Tara bubbles over with joy
and starts doing a "fancy footwork" to her dancing; other times she
will just stop and stare at Ganesh (the elephant-headed Hindu god,
who removes obstacles on the spiritual path) or one of the other gods.
Then she'll remember where she is and start dancing again.

2. *Practice it every day, and read spiritual stories to children, including stories
   about saints.* With my daughter, I make spirituality a natural part of our
   day as well as an area of special emphasis. We meditate together daily
   and close every day with evening prayers and a chant of love to God.
   On a recent family outing to the beach, Tara and I made a Shiva
   lingham [statue] from the sand, did a mini *puja* [devotional ceremony]
   of saying "Om Namah Shivaya" and offering flowers. Then Tara gave
   the *lingham* a bath and he dissolved back into the sand. Tara said, "We
   made the biggest Shiva *lingham* in the world—well, at least it's the
   biggest one on the beach." Her dad started doing this with her when
   she was about four. Instead of making sand castles, they would make
   Shiva together (sometimes they make sand castles, too). We always read
   stories together before she goes to bed. Stories about the lives of
   Hindu and Buddhist gods and saints are some of our favorites. She
   loves to read about Baby Krishna and all the mischief he would get
   into. It seems reassuring to her that even Krishna, who was an incarna-
   tion of Vishnu, sometimes got into trouble. In addition, so many children's books are filled with tales of true friendship, loyalty, love, and
   kindness, which are all spiritual values. We are careful about what television shows she watches, and her dad, her auntie, or I usually sit with
   her when she watches a program or video. A parent can help a child
   pick out the good qualities in people and why they are admirable and,
   likewise, why we don't want to be like the nasty people. We avoid her
   exposure to violence of any kind, and, again, living this is very important. We don't hit, spank, or use physical violence against children. We

also try not to use words as weapons, and don't yell and shout or say mean things to her. Sometimes you need to raise your voice in urgency, such as "Don't run into the road!" But most problems can be talked about with a calm voice.

3. *Talk with your child about kindness, generosity, compassion, love, and sharing.* Young children are so eager to learn. I make a point of talking often about values that are important to us. We talk about the things we see happen around us, like people arguing at a store or a mom slapping her child out of frustration. We explain that we don't think this is a good way to treat people, but try to teach compassion for the difficulty in people's lives. We emphasize "live and let live" or tolerance, rather than judging people. Hindu philosophy maintains that all souls will attain liberation but are at different levels of evolution.

4. *Visit spiritual places and people: lamas, saints, and ashrams.* We have many saints and holy people visit us at Shoshoni, so Tara has had the blessings of many holy people. Returning from a recent visit to a saint's ashram, Tara was so inspired that she said, "Mommy, I want you to take me to the temple one hour every day!" Living at the ashram, she goes to daily *arati* for about thirty minutes and then ten minutes of meditation. In the evening, we sit together in our family shrine room. She practices for about an hour over the course of the day—at five years old! Each person and each child is different. The amount of time is not the most important thing. I think the time spent in devotion should be fun and enjoyable, but there are days when it is an exercise in self-discipline, when she is less than enthusiastic. I try not to force or push too hard. I don't want her to reject spirituality someday like so many people who are forced to do it when they are children.

5. *I have the idea of awakening the spirituality within her rather than giving her something.* Recently she was playing intently as I sang devotional songs in our Ma shrine. Then she began rocking the rocking chair vigorously, observing how far the pillow would slap back and forth. After a while, I shot her a stern glance and suggested she practice mantra. She sat down, groaning with resistance, and fiddled with her fingers. Later that day I brought up her behavior. She felt she shouldn't have gotten

in trouble because she was being happy in the shrine. I agreed that it is wonderful to be happy, but that I thought maybe she was doing science experiments in the shrine—testing how far forward the pillow will slap—instead of practicing her mantra and meditating. At this, we both laughed. I told her that while I think science experiments are great, in the shrine we practice loving the gods. Then I told her that when I was pregnant with her, I often felt she was talking to me. I felt her instructing me on how to be her mom. She made me promise to her that I would help her remember who she really was, that she was the inner self. She seemed to be telling me that this was why she was coming to me, why I would be her mom, because I would help her remember. In Shavite philosophy, our true nature is consciousness, being, and bliss. We simply need to awaken to our true nature. I concluded, "When I tell you to meditate and repeat mantra, I am just following your instructions. You made me promise to help you remember your true nature. You see, really you are the boss. I am just doing what you told me to do." Again we both laughed. It seems to me that of all the things we can do in this world, we have the ability to make the most difference in the children. Loving them and helping them wake up to the radiant self in their own being is the great joy of being a parent.

DR. JAY GORDON, author of *Good Food Today, Great Kids Tomorrow.* Our daughter, Simone, is thirteen. When she was younger and more compliant with my desire to hike nearly every day, we'd celebrate holidays at the midpoint of a hike through the hills in Southern California. We'd look long and peacefully at the marvels of nature within easy view: mountains and valleys and the ocean and occasionally a wild animal or two. We'd talk about how everything came into existence and the likelihood of a Supreme Being in charge of the universe. Later, during her early years in school, my wife and I talked about variations on the Golden Rule and having a sense of treating people with kindness and respect. We celebrate some religious holidays with a congregation and some at home or with friends.

BRIGITTE MARS, herbalist, author of numerous books, including *Elder,* **and the CD-ROM** *Herbal Pharmacy,* **and mother of two daughters, now grown.** One of the best times to fill your children with spirit is when observing some grand beauty of the world—like taking them outside to see the moonrise or a beautiful sunset and telling them about our Creator and that we are loved. Also, pray with your children before bed, and give thanks often. Let them know that you can talk to God as a friend, and that praying does not have to be anything memorized.

PART 2

THE NATURAL APPROACH TO COMMON CHILDHOOD ILLNESSES

Chapter 6

A Stay-Healthy Plan for the Cold and Flu Season

When my daughter started preschool, it was the first time she was exposed to large groups of children (and they can carry viruses) every day. After talking to numerous natural medicine experts, it became clear that protecting her from the onslaught of viruses should have begun before she started school, and I needed to become more vigilant about her diet.

ANTIBIOTICS, DIET, AND THE IMMUNE SYSTEM

Every parent must understand how the body's immune system works and why the immune system isn't fully developed in young children. When the body is exposed to a virus, the immune system kicks into action with its multilayered defense team. First, white blood cells rush to the endangered area to attack the invading microorganisms. Next, the lymphatic system moves debris and microorganisms to the lymph nodes, where lymphocytes, the more concentrated white blood cells, are waiting to produce antibodies to the invading microorganisms. Here also are large cells called macrophages, the immune system's garbage collectors, which eat up the offending microorganisms and debris.

The two main types of lymphocytes are B cells and T cells. B cells mature in the bone marrow and produce antibodies to bind to specific antigens.

Once this happens, a B memory cell is produced that stimulates immunity in the future against the same particular microorganisms. An infant's immune system is immature; however, a newborn has an acquired immunity from the mother, which lasts for the first three months of life. Breast-feeding provides the infant with additional maternal antibodies and immune-enhancing factors to build immunity.

A baby's lymphocytes aren't capable of producing all the antibodies necessary to fight disease. The baby acquires this ability over the first few years of life as she is exposed to viruses and bacteria. These offending microorganisms cause the child's lymphocytes to make antibodies and memory cells so that when she comes into contact with those microorganisms again, the body will mount an immune response more quickly.

Understanding this process makes it clear why young children get sick so often. There are ways to reduce the duration and frequency of your child's illnesses, however. Kim Kelly, N.D., L.M., a practitioner in Seattle, Washington, treats hundreds of sick children during cold and flu season. "If your children are healthy, they may get sick when first exposed to viruses, especially at day care or preschool, but they'll get over it quickly and won't get sick again for a long time," she explains. "By strengthening your child with natural remedies and diet, and by helping them get well without antibiotics, they'll be stronger afterward."

Though antibiotics may help momentarily, they weaken the immune system in the long run, and the child may pick up another virus more quickly. Kelly suggests giving one dose of glycerin-based liquid echinacea and 500 milligrams of vitamin C—which plays an important role in immune response to infection—daily for three days prior to starting school or getting an immunization. When an infection strikes, special cells in the immune system release large amounts of oxidizing materials that can be toxic to other cells. Researchers have found that activation of these toxin-releasing cells promotes the consumption of vitamin C in the body, suggesting that high concentrations of the vitamin may protect against the toxins' harmful effects. Other studies have shown that vitamin C enhances the production of interferon, a protein excreted by cells when exposed to a virus. Interferon is believed to work in the early stages of viral exposure by preventing the multiplication of the virus until other facets of the immune system take over.

Echinacea also has a reputation as an immune enhancer. For centuries, herbalists have prescribed it to fight infection. Numerous European studies have shown that the herb boosts immunity by increasing the body's production of disease-fighting white blood cells. Before the discovery of antibiotics, echinacea was one of the most widely prescribed medicines in the United States.

Herbs and vitamins are not the only prescription for a healthy immune system. Natural practitioners agree that you must reduce your child's sugar intake drastically so that his immune system isn't depressed and can fight these viruses. A carbohydrate-based diet is another ticket to lowered immunity. Pasta and cereal don't contain the required nutritional elements, such as minerals, needed by children who are growing rapidly. Children need to eat a minimum of two servings of protein and plenty of fresh vegetables every day.

Earl Mindell, R.Ph., Ph.D., author of *Parents' Nutrition Bible,* agrees on the importance of a healthy diet. He advises parents not to serve dairy foods to their children during cold and flu season because dairy foods increase mucus production in the body. "Cow's milk is absolutely the worst food possible for any child who's ever had an ear infection. And numerous studies have made it obvious that the standard American diet, with its processed foods and sugar, depresses the immune system."

Children are smart, and they'll understand when you explain why certain foods are healthier than others. "Tell them that fast food from McDonald's isn't real food," Mindell explains. "You must teach them. They can splurge every now and then. But you, as a parent, must build the foundation of their understanding of food."

Mindell, also an advocate of herbs and vitamin supplements, is disturbed that most pediatricians offer antibiotics instead of recommending natural remedies. His remedies for keeping children healthy, especially through the virus season, include a diet with little or no sugar, a teaspoon of fish liver oil each day, odorless garlic tablets, vitamin C, and a daily multiple vitamin and mineral supplement. He also suggests giving echinacea in tincture form at the first sign of cold or flu.

"When I was a child, my mother gave me a teaspoon of fish liver oil each day, and it contained so many nutrients that boost the immune system," remembers Mindell. "Mothers today aren't doing that, and it's because their pediatricians aren't telling them about its benefits. Even garlic, such a simple, effective remedy, can be given daily in odorless tablets."

Garlic has been shown to have antibiotic properties as well as antibacterial properties beneficial in healing a chronic runny nose. Sugar consumption, especially refined white sugar, dramatically inhibits immune function by reducing the ability of neutrophils, the white blood cells primarily responsible for defense against bacteria, to engulf and destroy bacteria. In fact, studies show that sugar inhibits the lymphocytes' ability to produce antibodies to invading microorganisms.

IT'S WORTH THE EFFORT

Health practitioner Janet Zand encourages parents to boost their children's immunity before school starts. She advocates a blend of herbs including echinacea, goldenseal, and astragalus taken two or three times a week during cold and flu season, in addition to a healthy diet that includes hot vegetable soups, chicken soups laced with astragalus, and adequate mineral supplementation.

To build immunity, Zand also suggests the herb American ginseng, given in liquid form once or twice a week during the winter months. (However, because it is considered a "warming" herb, it should *never* be given when the child has a fever or other signs of an acute infection.) American ginseng is believed to help strengthen the body's overall constitution and relieve fatigue after an illness.

Zand recommends liquid colloidal minerals daily as well as 150 milligrams of vitamin C with bioflavonoids, and one dose of beta-carotene daily during the winter months. She also suggests a no-fried-foods diet, especially during cold and flu season, since those foods have been proven to lower immunity, as do foods high in sugar.

Simple as it sounds, she also advises washing hands regularly, a basic element of good hygiene to prevent the spread of infection.

It's important for parents to understand that their efforts can make a big difference in their children's health. "A small effort made up front to prevent illness saves lots of sleepless nights for everyone later on," says Zand.

PREVENTING COLDS AND FLU:
EXPERT ADVICE*

Janet Zand's recommendations:
- Low-sugar, no-fried-foods diet
- Lots of physical activity
- Drink plenty of clean water
- Fresh chicken and/or vegetable soup made with astragalus
- Regular hand washing
- One dose of liquid echinacea, goldenseal, and astragalus three times a week
- One dose of liquid American ginseng twice a week
- One dose of liquid colloidal minerals daily
- One dose of beta-carotene daily
- 150 milligrams of vitamin C with bioflavonoids daily

Kim Kelly's recommendations:
- One dose of glycerin-based liquid echinacea and 500 milligrams of vitamin C daily for three days before starting school or getting immunized
- Low-sugar diet (restrict fruit juice)
- Two servings of protein and plenty of fresh vegetables daily

Earl Mindell's recommendations:
- No dairy foods
- No processed foods
- Low-sugar diet
- One teaspoon of fish liver oil daily
- One odorless garlic tablet daily
- 100 milligrams of vitamin C daily
- Multiple vitamin and mineral supplement daily
- Liquid echinacea at first sign of cold or flu

Note: These dosages are for children age four and older.

Chapter 7

When Your Child Has a Fever

I t's 2 A.M. and your child's fever is approaching 103 degrees. What do you do? Indeed, witnessing your child's soaring temperature may be one of the scariest moments you will face as a new parent.

As frightening as a fever can be, it is actually the body's natural way of healing itself. White blood cells, which defend the body against invading viruses, work more effectively with an elevated body temperature. Furthermore, viruses and bacteria do not survive well under such circumstances. Most fevers are the body's normal reaction to an infection, usually viral in nature.

In adults, the degree of the fever may reflect the severity of the illness. In a child, this usually is not the case. A child with a cold can have a 104-degree fever. A child with bacterial pneumonia can have a 100-degree fever. Poor appetite, fatigue, and irritability probably indicate infection better than a fever does.

Controlling a fever is helpful for two reasons. First, children are very uncomfortable when they have a fever. They don't sleep, drink, or eat well. Bringing down a fever gently may help your child sleep, which is important for healing to take place and imperative to avoid dehydration. Second, bringing a fever down will help you diagnose your child's illness. A child with a 103-degree fever, regardless of whether he has a cold or pneumonia, will look and feel very sick. The child with a cold looks and feels much better when his fever is brought down. The child with pneumonia, however, will feel and look sick even when the fever is down. And remember, a fever of

105 degrees or higher, or lasting more than two days, must be evaluated by your doctor.

My physician, a conventional M.D., always told me not to use Tylenol (acetaminophen) unless my child's temperature reached 103 degrees. I've done a lot of reading on the dangers of using over-the-counter drugs such as Tylenol, and I've learned that it doesn't take many days of ingesting Tylenol (or other conventional fever remedies) to endanger the liver. These drugs put a tremendous strain on the liver as it tries to cleanse the blood of the after-effects of acetaminophen. They also suppress the exact body function that is helping the body to heal: fever.

From observing my daughter, I have learned that it's best to let your child's fever burn for the first twenty-four to forty-eight hours of an illness, resorting to drugs such as Tylenol as seldom as possible within that time frame. If you and your child are able to do this, the illness usually will be shorter and less severe than if you stifle the fever from the beginning.

I also have found that administering homeopathic remedies at the first sign of a fever can help bring it down gently. (See chapter 11 on homeopathy.) I've often used aconite and belladonna for this reason, and they have worked well for me. Also, be sure your child is getting plenty of fluids. Herbal teas (such as peppermint/chamomile), diluted juices, and water are essential to help the body cope with fever and can help reduce it. Powdered vitamin C mixed with juice is another natural way to help bring down the fever. The herb white willow, given in tincture form and dropped into juice or water, can help immensely. I often use a liquid herbal formula made by Herbs for Kids, which contains peppermint, elder, and yarrow for reducing fevers.

One of the most effective remedies I've discovered is to make a pot of mint/chamomile tea and dilute it until tepid. Dip a washcloth into the brew and rub it lightly over your child's head, legs, and feet. This is a gentle way to help control a rising fever. Remember never to use ice cold water or alcohol, since these can cause a rebound effect, making the fever go up even higher.

EXPERT ADVICE

I asked natural healer Michael Murray, N.D., coauthor of *The Encyclopedia of Natural Medicine,* to share his insights into childhood fevers and natural remedies.

Q: *Many natural healers have told me that it's good for a child to run a fever because it helps fight the infection. Do you believe this?*

Murray: Yes, within reason. As parents, we never like to see our children uncomfortable. But a fever is "just what the doctor ordered" to help fight an infection. Numerous studies have documented the immune-enhancing effects of a fever. It basically amplifies the immune response. However, too high a fever should be avoided.

Q: *How high can a mother let the fever go before she reaches for the Tylenol?*

Murray: I would recommend that before reaching for the Tylenol or any other fever reducer, a mother or father should consult a physician to identify the cause of the fever, especially in children under the age of two years. The presence of a fever is a sign that something is going on; don't ignore or discount it in a young child, as it could be the harbinger of a serious infection like meningitis or a blood or kidney infection. If the cause of the fever is relatively benign, like the common cold, it is unlikely that the fever is going to get above 102 degrees Fahrenheit, which seems to be a cutoff point as to when a child starts to be really uncomfortable.

Q: *What do you do with your children when they run a fever?*

Murray: We use Esberitox, made by Phyto Pharmica, and vitamin C— those little tablets from Hylands are great for kids—to boost the immune system. Esberitox is the most popular echinacea product in Germany. In addition to containing standardized extracts of the roots from two species of echinacea—purpurea and pallida—Esberitox also contains special extracts of *Thuja occidentalis* and *Baptisia tinctoria*—two other herbal medicines valued for their immune-enhancing activity. Esberitox also has the most solid scientific studies showing it to be beneficial during infections, including the common cold. In addition to positive studies in adults, clinical studies have shown Esberitox to be quite effective in preventing colds, flu, and ear infections in children in day care and nurseries. One of the real advantages of Esberitox is that it comes in good-tasting, small tablets suitable for children. We use those little vitamin C tablets from Hylands to provide 100 milligrams every two hours during an active infection.

Naturopathic physician Frank Ervolino of Seattle, Washington, shares his experiences treating children with fevers. The father of two young children, Dr. Ervolino received his training from Bastyr University in Seattle.

"Fever is that mystical demon that makes one earn the right to be called a parent. Fevers almost always occur on Saturday or Sunday night, when parents are essentially on their own. I remember getting a call late one Saturday night from a neighbor whose child was suddenly very ill. There was a tone of urgency to her voice. 'Frank, Kayla is very sick and I'm very concerned. She's got a fever, I think.' To a doctor, the determination of a fever is a black-or-white issue; either you have a fever or you don't. I asked, 'Did you take her temperature?' 'No' was her sheepish reply.

"If there is one thing a parent should have on hand, it is a formidable array of thermometers. Forget all the fancy backpacks and early child development gizmos. Get yourself a digital ear thermometer and a couple of mercury thermometers, as well as one of the new gadgets like a pacifier thermometer. Taking the temperature is the parents' responsibility, and it gives them a wealth of information they and their doctor can use.

"I went to Kayla's house and found her lying quietly in her bed with a red face and a very hot forehead. I took her temperature, and it wasn't easy. I was using an ear thermometer, and as soon as I tried to put it in her ear for the required two seconds, she suddenly came alive, screaming and thrashing about.

"The first thing that crossed my mind was an ear infection, and the second was delirium. The mother held her down, and I took my reading . . . 104 degrees. I told the mother, and she started to get an ashen look on her face. She asked, 'Should I take her to the emergency room?' I told her to relax. I explained that even though her daughter was very sick, her body's immune system was doing its job.

"Then the dad arrived and expressed his concern. 'What about that temperature? Is it too high?' I told him, 'No, it's OK for a child to have a temperature as high as 105 degrees, but at 104 degrees we should be doing something like using cool compresses to help her remain comfortable.' Kayla's father applied cool compresses while I wrote instructions for Mom to take her temperature at least every half hour, and to administer some catnip tea, which would keep the fever at a more acceptable level, under 104 degrees.

"A fever is a change in the body's temperature set point, and it is mainly brought on by the white blood cells attacking a bacterial infection in the body. As the bacteria is destroyed, interleukin-1 is released into the bloodstream and is then detected in the brain, causing the brain's thermostat to be turned up. It is a sign of a very active immune system.

"In viral infections, it is thought that the fever raises the body's temperature to a level that harms the virus's ability to stay alive. A fever is not a sign of deterioration of a child's condition. In a mild illness, the child will appear alert and active, and be able to smile and eat. Moderately ill children will be fussy or irritable but consolable. Severely ill children will appear listless, cannot be consoled, will not eat; they may be vomiting or have abdominal distention, mild delirium, and even seizures. Severely ill children need to be under a physician's care.

"Danger signs for a fever are a temperature over 40 degrees Celsius, or 104 degrees Fahrenheit; the child acts confused, loses consciousness, starts to twitch, or seems hot on one side of the body and cold on the other.

"What happened to Kayla? I got a call from her mom the next day, and she was still running that high fever. I gave her some elder flower syrup, which is a medicine children will take while sick, and some Chinese herbal medicine. The elder flower syrup is used to mask the taste of the Chinese herbs. I called again that evening, and Kayla was still very ill with a high temperature. I went to their house and prepared some herbal tea for her condition and gave it to her as an enema. An herbal enema is the best way to dose a very sick young child. It rehydrates them, gives them about a three-day dose of herbs, and is absorbed by the intestines very quickly. Her parents were amazed at how compliant she was—and how it didn't make a mess. She actually absorbed a half-cup of tea. I use those little blue syringe bulbs they send home with a new baby from the hospital, and a little olive oil to lube the opening.

"The next day I got a call from the parents; Kayla's fever had broken and she was doing very well. If the fever does not break in a reasonable amount of time, I will use acetaminophen to break it. It is a very good use for an otherwise overused medicinal.

"You want the child to have a fever for a while. If you break it right away, you confuse the immune system, and you can get an echo pattern wherein the child is intermittently sick all winter. I see this all the time in my practice, and it is very hard to resolve. I also feel that parents who are fear-based in their approach to fever, and exercise too much control over the child's body, transfer that fear to the child.

"Grief and fear are the emotions of the lungs and kidneys in Chinese medicine; these two organs are often behind allergies and asthma. Asthma is on the rise in young children in America so much that HMOs are alarmed and seeking new ways to address asthma. I feel that a parent who educates himself or herself on how to deal with the child in times of illness will give the child a certain confidence. That calm confidence may prevent negative emotions from having an adverse effect on the child's life."

SOME HELPFUL HINTS FOR COPING WITH A FEVER

1. Homeopathic remedies such as aconite and belladonna.

2. Vitamin C (in small tablets made by Hylands).

3. Push liquids, especially water, peppermint/chamomile tea, or catnip tea.

4. Try an herbal tincture made by Herbs for Kids containing peppermint, elder, and yarrow.

5. Dip a rag into cool peppermint/chamomile tea and rub it lightly across the child's head, legs, and feet.

6. Try a chewable echinacea herb tablet called Esberitox (made by Phyto Pharmica).

Chapter 8

Healthy Skin

Natural Personal Care for Kids

I t's easy to forget that the skin is the body's largest organ, and whatever we put on it is absorbed into our bodies. This is especially true for children and infants. Never put a lotion, cream, or soap on your child that you wouldn't want her to put into her mouth. That may sound far-fetched, but it gives you an idea of how the skin works.

When your baby is born, remember that her skin is perfect and doesn't need scrubbing with soap. My daughter had only water baths for many years. There's simply no reason to use soap unless your child has been playing in the dirt. In that case, use only the gentlest, plant-based, and chemical-free soaps and shampoos that you can find, such as those made by a company called Weleda.

Your first foray into skin care with your child probably will be diaper rash. Keep your child's bottom as dry as possible by changing her often and letting her "air out" by being diaper-free whenever possible. Avoid using rubber or plastic pants. We used cotton balls dipped in a baking soda/water solution to eliminate diaper rash quickly.

Many herbal salves made for diaper rash work quite well. We used one made with chamomile and other soothing herbs. Natural baby powder is free of irritating talc, which, according to Ruth Winter's *A Consumer's Dictionary of Cosmetic Ingredients,* has a chemical composition similar to asbestos. Natural powders are formulated with French white clay, arrowroot, and herbs such as slippery elm and aloe vera.

Cradle cap, a condition in which patches of scales form over the scalp, is a common skin problem in infancy, and it is a sign of essential fatty acid deficiency. Massaging the scalp with flaxseed oil, then combing out with a fine-tooth comb, usually will eliminate the problem.

EXPERT ADVICE

Here, I've asked herbalist and author Brigitte Mars to answer questions about baby's and children's skin problems. She always tells parents to be sure to avoid mineral oil, synthetic fragrances, and artificial colors. Calendula is an excellent, gentle baby herb for topical skin care.

Diaper Rash

Diaper rash may occur when either the mother's or baby's diet has become overly acidic. It may indicate that tomatoes, citrus products, sweets, and even fruits are being overconsumed or becoming aggravating. Keep the baby's bottom diaper-free as much as possible. Avoid using rubber or plastic pants as well as disposable diapers. If you launder your own cloth diapers, add ¼ cup apple cider vinegar to the final rinse water. Apply a soothing calendula salve to the baby's bottom. Many parents report that an application of plain yogurt to the baby's bottom has helped to clear up a persistent rash. Also consider giving the baby an acidophilus supplement that is formulated for infants.

Eczema and Psoriasis

Because these two conditions tend to change and spread, they often are likened to "wind invasion" in Oriental medicine. Eczema is characterized by dry, rashy areas that itch. Psoriasis involves rapidly growing cells that come to the skin's surface before they are fully mature. It manifests as skin patches that may be red, thickened, and covered with silvery scales that usually do not itch. It is considered more stubborn than eczema. New skin grows back about five times faster than old skin can be shed.

People who suffer from psoriasis tend to be on the run, moving rapidly, like their skin growth. Foods to avoid include dairy products, citrus, tomatoes, peanut butter, fried foods, and hydrogenated oils. Exposure to chemicals can also affect our skin in a negative way.

In both eczema and psoriasis, it is helpful to cool the blood and skin. A tea or extract of burdock root, raw dandelion root, Oregon grape root, and yellow dock root, would be excellent. Other remedies include liquid flaxseed oil taken daily (see your practitioner for dosages). An alternative is capsules of evening primrose oil. Avoid contact with chemicals on the skin.

Dry cleaning fluid, bubble baths, and cleaning products all can be contributing factors to skin problems. Be careful of nylon, suede, wool, and synthetic fibers. It may help to put 1 cup apple cider vinegar to the final rinse of a washload to neutralize possible irritants. Place baking soda, apple cider vinegar, or two handfuls of oatmeal wrapped and tied inside a cloth to your bathwater. A folk remedy worthy of trying is to apply raw potato juice (made in a juicer) to the affected area.

If more infants were breast-fed, it would help cut down on the incidence of eczema and psoriasis. However, it is possible that a nursing baby could have allergies to a food his mother is consuming, so she may need to alter her diet somewhat to eliminate the possible culprits. Children with eczema may benefit from extra cuddling at night before bed. Massage is also a good way to soothe tension.

Vitamins A, C, and E, as well as zinc, may also be helpful. Look for salves to apply topically that include aloe vera, burdock, calendula, chickweed, comfrey, echinacea, goldenseal, plantain, and St. John's wort.

Swimming in the ocean may be helpful to both eczema and psoriasis. Scratching itchy skin can cause more irritation and make one more prone to infection. Consider keeping the fingernails very short and even wearing gloves to sleep to prevent scratching.

Cradle Cap

Cradle cap is a type of infantile seborrheic dermatitis caused by overactive sebaceous glands or, in some cases, a yeast called *Pityrosporum ovale*. It is not caused by poor hygiene.

Babies may have flaking of the skin and redness on the scalp and head and also under the arms and groin area. It is not itchy, contagious, or painful and tends to bother the parents more than the child. It usually begins between two weeks and three months of age and can last until the toddler stage.

At night, rub the baby's scalp with olive, wheat germ, or sesame oil scented with a few drops of lavender or rosemary essential oil. Avoid using harsh soaps and shampoos on the baby. The baby's scalp can be washed with a tepid tea of burdock root, chamomile, chickweed, meadowsweet, or violet leaf. Leave the tea on the scalp. When it is dry, apply cocoa butter to soften the crusts.

Another remedy is to fill a cloth bag (cheesecloth works well) with oatmeal, tie it closed, and use it to wash the scalp. Use a fine-tooth comb to loosen the afflicted spots. The nursing mom should add some flaxseed oil and burdock root tea to her diet to help metabolize as well as control any fungus growth.

Ear Infections

Ear infections are the number-one reason why parents take children to a pediatrician, and why they give their children antibiotics. Fortunately, there are other options. A twenty-four-hour course of garlic/mullein oil in the ears along with oral dosages of echinacea, goldenseal, and vitamin C, and a child's earache may be cured.

Frank Ervolino, a naturopathic physician in Seattle, Washington, shares his experience in treating children with ear infections.

"Probably the most perplexing pediatric condition encountered by general practice physicians is otitis media. The first time I saw a case was early on in my practice. A little boy was brought to me with an acute case of otitis media and I gave him the standard protocol: garlic/mullein ear drops, echinacea with hydrastis, and elder flower tea. He cleared up right away and I thought, *No sweat. I'm real good at this stuff.* Beginner's luck is what I call it now. Over the years I have seen cases of otitis media, both chronic and acute, that have brought me to my knees, figuratively speaking. But in each case I learned a little more about the art of healing and what it means to bring out the healing power within.

"Take the little girl with multiple attacks of acute otitis media with a skyrocketing fever of up to 105 degrees. She was only three years old and her parents were very loving. Both worked, and she spent her days in a very nice day care center. The attacks would come on suddenly and force the mother to take many days off work. I tried the usual protocol mentioned above, but it did not work. Then I tried the homeopathic remedies— chamomile, belladonna, aconitum, and pulsatilla. The attacks still kept coming. The father was losing his patience, and, being a working father myself,

I could empathize. He wanted to take action that would restore control over the situation: ear tubes. I told him that might stop the acute attacks for now, but it didn't address the larger problem of finding the cause. He told me I had two more weeks to work a miracle. I hit the books, as I am known to do, and found a perfect description of this little girl in a book on Chinese acupuncture and herbs.

"In my interview, I found out that the mother had been ill often and very tired during her pregnancy. She also had had a hard time recovering from her pregnancy. The little girl had been very frail during her first two years of life, and when she got sick she would have alternating chills and fever. Nothing tasted good to her when she was sick. The mother also told me that her little girl was a worrier and had some separation anxiety when she took her to the day care center each day, but once mom was gone, the child was fine. I asked the mother how she felt about taking her daughter to day care every day, and I saw tears well up in her eyes. She said she was devastated over the thought of someone else raising her daughter during these most precious days, but they needed her income because they had just bought a new home. Purchasing a home in Seattle is a far more expensive proposition than in many other areas of the country.

"This is what I came up with. This little girl had a weakened immune system, which allowed the invasion into her body of whatever pathogen was causing her otitis. The pathogen was getting deeper than it should in a normal person. For those of you thinking about allergic reactions in the eustachian tube blocking the tube and allowing bacteria to form, this is still applicable because her intestines are also part of the immune system, or house components of the immune system, and they are responsible for keeping out large proteins, which will cause an immune reaction in the tube. In Chinese medicine, this is called a Shaoyang syndrome. It is characterized by alternating chills and fever, a bitter taste in the mouth, no appetite, and irritability. We used a formula called *Xiao Chai Hu Tang* and gave it to her by masking the taste in honey/loquat syrup. She recovered nicely, but the real advance in her health came when I explained to the mother that her pain of letting go of her daughter was an emotion that in Chinese medicine belongs to the lungs; and this is the source of the immune system in traditional Chinese medicine. I told her that her daughter was picking up on this and having her own lungs compromised by the anxiety.

"My recommendation was for her to take a few days off each month to spend time with her daughter and develop a long-term plan to stay home full-time if she really wanted that. I then prescribed a spearmint-flavored astragalus glycerite for the little girl to tonify her lung *qi,* and an herbal formula for the mother to alleviate her anxiety. Two years later, the little girl has not had any recurrence of the otitis media, the husband got a promotion at work, and his wife was able to stay home with their daughter. When I look back at this, the most rewarding part of the experience is getting people to wish for something that is for the good of all involved and putting it out there in the universe so it can happen. To me, that is real healing."

SIX THINGS TO CONSIDER FOR EAR INFECTIONS

1. Garlic/mullein oil drops in the ear.

2. Vitamin C.

3. Echinacea/goldenseal herb tincture.

4. Elimination of all dairy from the diet, since this creates mucus.

5. Babies who are breast-fed have significantly fewer ear infections than bottle-fed babies.

6. Homeopathic remedies such as aconite, belladonna, and pulsatilla.

Chapter 9

Natural Remedies for Children's and Infants' Common Complaints*

Note: For more information about using aromatherapy, see page 154. Always dilute aromatherapy oils with vegetable oil before applying to skin—unless otherwise advised. If you are using an aromatherapy treatment, wait an hour before administering a homeopathic remedy, or else the strong scent may interfere with the action of the homeopathic medicine.

GENTLE REMEDIES FOR INFANTS

Colic

Aromatherapy

Dill—a carminitive; dilute 1 drop in 1 tablespoon sweet almond oil; massage tummy.

Homeopathy

Belladonna—if baby's tummy feels hot; baby is constipated; baby has spasms that come and go quickly.

---

*By contributing author Lara Pizzorno, M.A. (Div.), M.A. (Lit.), L.M.T.

Carbo vegetalis—if baby has a pale face, distended upper abdomen, cold legs from the knee down.

Chamomilla—best remedy when infants are teething; abdomen is tender and distended; child vomits or has green, foul-smelling diarrhea.

Magnesia phosphorica—for bloating, burping, gas, relieved by applying warm compresses and bending into fetal position.

Herbal Medicine

Chamomile, peppermint, fennel tea, or a mixture of all three—taken by the mother if breast-feeding, ½ cup daily if given via bottle.

Supplement

Probiotics—taken by the mother if breast-feeding; if not, give ⅛ to ¼ teaspoon per day in formula.

Diaper Rash

Aromatherapy

Chamomile German—gentle, soothing antibacterial, antiseptic, disinfectant, and anti-inflammatory.

Homeopathy

Calcarea carbonica—for an infant who tends to perspire on the head and feet, and whose sweat and stools smell sour.

Sulphur—for red, sore rash.

Thuja—for persistent rash.

Herbal Medicine

Calendula lotion or gel—soothing and healing.

Evening primrose oil or lotion—anti-inflammatory.

Supplements

Probiotics—taken by the mother if breast-feeding; if not, give ⅛ to ¼ teaspoon per day in formula.

Cornstarch—absorbs moisture between diaper changes.

Baking soda—mix 1 tablespoon baking soda in 4 ounces water and sponge on diaper area; baking soda's alkalinity will balance the acidity of urine and stool.

Fretfulness

Aromatherapy

Chamomile Roman—soothes nervous conditions and insomnia.

Geranium—soothes the emotions; a nerve tonic and gentle sedative.

Lavender—a relaxant, antidepressant, and gentle sedative.

Combine 1 drop of any of these oils in 1 tablespoon sweet almond oil, and massage into feet and spine. Or, make a blend of all three oils, then add 1 drop of the mixture to 1 tablespoon sweet almond oil.

Homeopathy

Chamomilla—if baby is fidgety; don't give with chamomile tea or chamomile essential oil, as they will cancel each other out.

Lycopodium—if baby is tired and irritable.

Herbal Medicine

Chamomile tea—taken by the mother if breast-feeding; ½ cup daily if given by bottle.

Supplement

Calcium and magnesium combination—taken by the mother if breast-feeding.

Teething

Aromatherapy

Chamomile Roman—antiseptic, calming, soothing. Add to bath or massage oil.

Chamomile German—high azulene content makes it especially soothing. Add to bath or massage oil.

Clove—a natural anesthetic. Blend 1 drop with 2 tablespoons flaxseed oil; rub gently on sore gums.

Homeopathy

Belladonna—for red, swollen, throbbing gums; red face; glassy eyes; heat, but little sweat.

Calcarea carbonica—if baby has a lot of fat and sweats profusely, especially on the head.

Chamomilla—if baby is irritable; demands something, then pushes it away; is temporarily relieved when held and rocked; may also have diarrhea or an earache. Don't give homeopathic chamomilla with chamomile tea or chamomile essential oil, as they will cancel each other out.

Silica—if baby is frail, delicate, often constipated.

Herbal Medicine

Licorice root powder—mix ⅛ teaspoon powder with enough water to make a paste, and pat on baby's gums.

REMEDIES FOR CHILDREN

Aches and Pains: Muscle Cramps, "Growing Pains"

Aromatherapy

Rosemary—if your child is over five years of age, stimulating rosemary is the oil of choice for all muscular complaints: sprains, strains, fatigue, pain from overexertion.

Lavender—best choice for children under five; lavender is a soothing, gentle relaxant.

Peppermint—a circulatory stimulant like rosemary, peppermint also soothes due to its cooling effect. Dilute with vegetable oil.

Too Much Exercise Massage Oil—combine 5 drops each of lavender, rosemary, and peppermint in 2 tablespoons organic, cold-pressed vegetable oil. Massage sore areas. Store in refrigerator.

Homeopathy

Arnica montana—first choice to prevent and reduce muscle aches from overexertion; if possible, begin taking 30 x potency prior to the activity. Take another dose every hour while awake for 24 hours if pain is still felt.

Rhus toxicodendron—if child feels achy at first, but better with continued motion.

Traumeel ointment—a combination remedy containing arnica, *Rhus tox,* plus several other helpful homeopathic medicines.

Supplement

Calcium and magnesium combination—calms and soothes the nervous system, relaxes blood vessels, which improves circulation and removal of lactic acid, a by-product of muscle cell metabolism that contributes to the achy feeling.

Acne and Pimples

Aromatherapy

Lemon—astringent, antibacterial, tones skin.

Lavender—antibacterial, antiseptic, soothes inflamed skin.

Tea tree oil—antibacterial, antifungal, antiviral, helps heal infected pores.

Homeopathy

A healthful whole-foods diet—adequate protein, fresh fruits and vegetables, and minimal saturated fat, refined flour, and sugar—along with a good skin-cleansing routine—is the foundation of healthy skin. Along with diet, the ups and downs of a teenager's emotions can also contribute to skin breakouts. If your child eats well and keeps her skin clean yet still has trouble, consult a homeopath for a constitutional remedy to help balance your teen's emotions.

Herbal Medicine

Aloe vera gel—soothes and heals red, inflamed skin.

Calendula gel—antiseptic, promotes healing of lesions.

Echinacea and goldenseal combination—echinacea is antiviral, goldenseal is antibacterial; both herbs boost immune response and help eliminate and prevent skin infections.

Supplements

Brewer's yeast—excellent source of B vitamins and trace minerals important for proper nervous system function and healthy skin.

Vitamin C—involved in the production of adrenal gland hormones, necessary for immune response to infections and for wound healing.

Beta-carotene—converted in the body to vitamin A, which strengthens mucus membranes and is a critical nutrient for immune and adrenal function.

Garlic—antiseptic, a natural antibiotic.

Omega-3 oils (such as evening primrose oil, flaxseed oil, cod liver oil, salmon oil)—essential fatty acids needed for healthy hair, skin, nails.

Calcium and magnesium combination—calms and balances the nervous system and improves circulation, thus improving waste removal from skin and delivery of nutrients to skin.

Zinc picolinate (10 to 15 milligrams)—a well-absorbed form of zinc, which is necessary for proper immune function, wound healing; adequate zinc prevents the formation of an inflammatory form of testosterone (dihydrotestosterone), which contributes to acne.

Allergies: Eczema, Hay Fever, Sinusitis, Asthma

ECZEMA

Aromatherapy

Chamomile German—its high azulene content makes it especially soothing. Mix 10 drops chamomile in 20 drops jojoba oil, plus 10 drops evening primrose oil, and apply to the affected area twice daily.

Homeopathy

Rhus toxicodendron—for dry, red, itchy areas in skinfolds, small blisters on skin surfaces; give if child feels better with warmth; a warm oatmeal bath also helps.

Sulphur—for a sweaty child who dislikes baths, throws off bed covers, wants skin exposed to cool air.

Urtica urens—for eczema that is dry and scaly. Available in ointment or gel.

Herbal Medicine

Calendula—ointment that is soothing and anti-inflammatory.

Comfrey—ointment that is soothing and anti-inflammatory.

Supplements

Omega-3 oils—anti-inflammatory and necessary for healthy skin; salmon or flaxseed oil are good sources.

Zinc—necessary for proper immune function and healthy skin.

Vitamin E—aids tissue healing; apply topically and give internally.

Beta-carotene—used in the body to form vitamin A, which is necessary for mucosal health, and promotes tissue healing.

HAY FEVER

Aromatherapy

Eucalyptus—anti-inflammatory, antiseptic, and analgesic; helps drain and heal inflamed sinuses.

Chamomile German—antiseptic, but most valued for its anti-inflammatory, soothing, calming effects.

Homeopathy

Allium cepa—for burning, watery discharge from the nose, bland tears, itchy eyes; administer if child is aggravated by warmth.

Arsenicum album—for burning tears and nasal discharge; give if child is thirsty but takes only small sips at a time, and feels better with warmth.

Euphrasia—for constant burning tears and bland nasal discharge; give if child feels worse at night, when lying down, and in open air.

Nux vomica—for constant nasal discharge during the day, congestion at night; administer if child is irritable, chilly, sneezing.

Pulsatilla—for bland yellow nasal discharge during the day, congestion at night; use if child is not thirsty but is moody and craves sympathy.

Herbal Medicine

Astragalus membranaceous—Chinese herb that helps strengthen the immune system.

Goldenseal—a natural antibiotic that also soothes mucus membranes.

Garlic—antibacterial, antiseptic herb.

Supplements

Omega-3 oils (such as evening primrose, flaxseed, cod liver, salmon oil)—promotes the expression of anti-inflammatory prostaglandins, thus decreasing inflammation; essential for proper immune function.

Zinc picolinate (10 to 15 milligrams)—trace mineral necessary for proper immune function.

Brewer's yeast—excellent source of B vitamins and trace minerals.

Vitamin C—antioxidant critical for proper immune function.

Quercetin—bioflavonoid with antihistamine activity that teams up with vitamin C.

Beta-carotene—precursor to vitamin A, necessary for healthy skin and mucosa.

SINUSITIS

Aromatherapy

Chamomile German—its high azulene content makes this oil an effective anti-inflammatory, plus it is antibacterial, antiseptic, and disinfectant.

Eucalyptus—a cooling and soothing anti-inflammatory, antiseptic, antibiotic, and analgesic oil.

Geranium—antiseptic, astringent, and sedative; helps shrink and calm inflamed sinuses.

Rosemary—astringent, antiseptic, helps shrink sinuses and promote drainage.

Homeopathy

Arsenicum—for throbbing and burning pains in the sinuses, sensitivity to light, nausea, vomiting; give if child feels better lying down with head raised on pillows and exposed to cool air.

Hepar sulphuris—for yellow or yellow-green nasal discharge.

Kali bichromicum—for thick, stringy white nasal discharge; administer if child feels better with warmth.

Mercurius—for a stuffy nose that isn't getting better, with thick, green, acrid, offensive-smelling nasal discharge.

Pulsatilla—for thick yellow or green nasal discharge; head pain that worsens when lying down; child also may have digestive problems.

Herbal Medicine

Echinacea and goldenseal combination (use for one week, then goldenseal alone can be used)—antiviral echinacea and antibacterial goldenseal both stimulate the immune response; goldenseal also soothes mucus membranes.

Garlic—antibacterial herb.

Supplements

Brewer's yeast—source of B vitamins and trace minerals.

Vitamin C—boosts immune function.

Quercetin—a bioflavonoid with antihistamine activity.

Beta-carotene—pro-vitamin A, heals mucus membranes, necessary for healthy skin.

Omega-3 oils (such as evening primrose oil, flaxseed oil, cod liver oil, salmon oil)—promotes the expression of anti-inflammatory prostaglandins, thus decreasing inflammation; essential for proper immune function.

Zinc picolinate (10 to 15 milligrams)—a well-absorbed form of zinc, which is a trace mineral essential for proper immune function.

ASTHMA

Aromatherapy

Lavender—antibiotic, antiseptic, antidepressant, sedative, circulatory stimulant; allays shock.

Geranium—antiseptic, astringent, sedative; helps shrink inflamed respiratory passages.

Homeopathy

Arsenicum—if child is tired, weak, restless, anxious, sensitive to cold.

Antimonium tantaricum—if the child is wheezing, has a tight feeling in the chest, and has difficulty coughing up mucus.

Chamomilla—if the asthma is triggered by anger and irritability.

Ipecac—for persistent nausea, a loose cough, rattling in the chest, difficulty expectorating.

Nux vomica—if the child feels full in the stomach or may have a feeling of choking.

Pulsatilla—for asthmatic breathing in warm, stuffy rooms; use if child feels better with cool air or craves sympathy.

Herbal Medicine

Astragalus membranaceous—Chinese herb that helps strengthen immune and lung function.

Chamomile—soothing, relaxant herb.

Licorice root—soothes lungs, helps strengthen adrenal function.

Goldenseal—natural antibiotic, boosts immune response.

Garlic—antibacterial herb.

Supplements

Brewer's yeast—excellent source of B vitamins and trace minerals, supports adrenal function, helps the body deal with stress.

Pantothenic acid—a B vitamin that supports adrenal function and the immune system.

B12—inadequate amounts of B12 have been linked to asthma.

Emergen-C—product from Alacer Corporation containing vitamin C, B vitamins, calcium, magnesium, potassium, sodium, manganese, chromium, and zinc; boosts immune function, helps body deal with stress.

Quercetin—a bioflavonoid with antihistamine activity.

Beta-carotene—pro-vitamin A, heals mucus membranes.

Omega-3 oils (such as evening primrose oil, flaxseed oil, cod liver oil, salmon oil)—essential fatty acids that reduce inflammatory response.

Magnesium—relaxes blood vessels, a natural bronchodilator.

Zinc picolinate (10 to 15 milligrams)—a well-absorbed form of zinc, which is a trace mineral essential for proper immune function.

Anxiety and Restlessness

Aromatherapy

Chamomile Roman—the species of chamomile most effective in treating nervous conditions and insomnia.

Geranium—sedative and nerve tonic.

Lavender—antidepressant, sedative.

Homeopathy

Arsenicum—if child is high-strung, nervous, easily frightened.

Chamomilla—if child throws temper tantrums; asks for, then refuses things; can't be satisfied.

Ignatia—if emotional or sexual abuse is suspected.

Nux vomica—if child is hyperactive, overly excitable, revved up, hypersensitive.

Rhus toxicodendron—if child is restless, confused, uneasy, especially at night.

Herbal Medicine

Chamomile—relaxant, sedative herb; don't give with homeopathic chamomilla, as they will cancel each other out.

Supplements

Calcium and magnesium combination—calcium and magnesium relax muscles, improve blood flow, soothe a keyed-up or stressed nervous system.

Brewer's yeast—excellent source of B vitamins and trace minerals, supports adrenal function, helps the body deal with stress.

Athlete's Foot

Aromatherapy

Healing Foot Bath—add 5 drops tea tree oil to 1 cup salt and place in a large bowl of water; soak the child's feet for at least 5 minutes daily. Dry feet well, then use Athlete's Foot Powder (see below).

Athlete's Foot Powder—add 10 drops tea tree oil a few drops at a time to a cup of dry green clay or cornstarch. Mix well and use to powder the feet before putting on cotton or wool (not nylon) socks.

Athlete's Foot Massage Oil—add 30 drops Tagetes to 2 tablespoons cold-pressed organic vegetable oil and use to massage feet before bed.

Homeopathy

Thuja—an effective homeopathic remedy for athlete's foot; use ointment as well as capsules.

Herbal Medicine

Garlic—a powerful fungicide; slice garlic and put in your child's socks; or add garlic slivers to cornstarch, let the mixture sit overnight, and use to dust feet and the inside of shoes.

Supplements

Emergen-C—product from Alacer Corporation containing vitamin C, B vitamins, calcium, magnesium, potassium, sodium, manganese, chromium, and zinc; boosts immune function, helps body deal with stress.

Quercetin with other bioflavonoids—anti-inflammatory, antiallergenic, works with vitamin C to boost immune function.

Beta-carotene—used by the body to produce vitamin A, heals mucus membranes, important for immune function.

Zinc picolinate—a well-absorbed form of zinc; zinc is essential for proper immune function; therapeutic dose is 15 to 20 milligrams twice daily for up to one week. Normal zinc intake should be 15 milligrams per day.

Boils; Burns; Cuts, Scrapes, and Puncture Wounds; Insect Bites and Stings

BOILS

Aromatherapy

Lavender—antibiotic, antiseptic, promotes healing, prevents scarring.

Tea tree oil—powerful antiseptic, antibiotic.

Chamomile—antibacterial, antiseptic, anti-inflammatory.

Boil Bathing Solution—combine 2 drops lavender, 2 drops tea tree oil, and 2 drops chamomile in a pint of hot water and use to bathe the area twice daily.

Homeopathy

Belladonna—brings down a bright red, hot, throbbing boil.

Hepar sulphuris—when a boil comes to a head or if it is extremely sensitive to the touch.

Silica—for boils that erupt after injury with a foreign body, such as a splinter.

Myristica—for a stubborn boil that won't open and drain.

Calcarea sulphurica—for a boil that isn't healing; give when the boil begins to drain.

Herbal Medicine

Echinacea and goldenseal combination—stimulates the immune system to clear infections. Echinacea boosts antiviral response for the first seven to ten days. Goldenseal is antiseptic and antibacterial and heals skin and mucus membranes.

Goldenseal—open a capsule, mix contents with a few drops of water to make a paste. Apply topically and cover with a bandage.

Ginger—soak a compress in ginger tea and apply to draw the boil to a head.

Usnea moss—effective against staphylococcus infection. Make a strong tea and use it to make a compress.

Herbal combination ointment—Super Salve, which contains chaparral, echinacea, hops, and usnea, is an excellent remedy.

Supplements

Beta-carotene—converted in the body to vitamin A, helps heal skin tissue.

Vitamin C with bioflavonoids—anti-inflammatory, boosts immune response, helps restore cell-wall integrity.

Zinc—aids in wound healing.

BURNS

Aromatherapy

Lavender—apply ice cold water for at least 10 minutes, then 2 drops neat (undiluted) lavender directly on the burn. Put 5 drops lavender on a dry, cold compress and cover the area.

Homeopathy

Calendula—for first-degree burns. Apply gel, spray, or diluted tincture.

Urtica urens—for first-degree burns. Take pill orally and/or apply gel or ointment topically.

Hypericum—for second-degree burns. Apply gel, spray, or diluted tincture externally; take internally if burns are on hands or feet, or if there are shooting pains.

Kali muriaticum—to prevent blistering. Crush a tablet in a little distilled water and apply topically.

Belladonna—use if the burn remains red and throbbing after initial treatment with a homeopathic remedy and the aromatic oil lavender, or the herbal remedy aloe vera.

Mercurius solubilis—use if the burn is becoming infected, and call your physician.

Herbal Medicine

Aloe vera gel—apply topically; aloe vera contains numerous compounds that facilitate wound healing, including vitamin C, vitamin E, and zinc. Glycoproteins in aloe vera block inflammatory mediators, thus reducing pain and swelling. Polysaccharides in aloe vera stimulate epidermal growth and repair.

Supplements

Beta-carotene—helps heal skin tissue.

Vitamin C with bioflavonoids—anti-inflammatory, boosts immune response, helps restore cell-wall integrity.

Zinc—aids in wound healing.

CUTS, SCRAPES, AND PUNCTURE WOUNDS

Aromatherapy

Lavender—a soothing, healing, yet powerful disinfectant.

Tea tree—a natural disinfectant that is antibacterial, antiviral, and antifungal.

Combination Cleansing Solution—cleanse cuts and scrapes with a solution of 8 drops lavender and 2 drops tea tree oil in a pint of lukewarm water; apply a drop of neat (undiluted) lavender to a bandage and cover the wound. If there is swelling, elevate the wounded area, dip a compress in ice water, wring it out, apply a drop of lavender to the compress, and place it on the wound.

Homeopathy

Calendula—applied topically, calendula ointment is the primary remedy for shallow cuts and scrapes. Once deeper cuts have begun to heal, calendula will speed up skin closure and healing.

Hypericum—homeopathic goldenseal, hypericum, applied topically, is the remedy of choice for deeper cuts; the pill form can be taken internally if the injury is causing sharp or shooting pains.

Arnica—taken internally, arnica helps with shock and reduces pain and swelling.

Ledum—taken internally, ledum is the primary remedy for puncture wounds and for hematoma (black-and-blue marks).

Traumeel ointment—a combination topical remedy for pain and inflammation associated with bruises.

Herbal Medicine

Aloe vera gel—aloe vera contains numerous compounds that facilitate wound healing, including vitamin C, vitamin E, and zinc. Other compounds in aloe vera block inflammatory mediators, thus reducing pain and swelling.

Goldenseal—a natural antibiotic. Open a capsule, mix contents with a few drops of water to make a paste, apply topically as a poultice, and cover with a bandage.

Supplements

Vitamin C with bioflavonoids—helps heal and strengthen blood vessel walls.

INSECT BITES AND STINGS

Aromatherapy

Chamomile—for bee and hornet stings, remove the stinger and apply a cold compress of chamomile for 15 to 20 minutes, then apply 1 drop neat (undiluted) chamomile.

Lavender—for wasp stings, put 2 drops lavender and 2 drops chamomile into 1 teaspoon of cider vinegar. Mix well and dab on bitten area. For spider bites, mix 3 drops lavender and 2 drops chamomile in 1 teaspoon alcohol and dab on area. For black widow bites, apply 10 drops neat undiluted lavender to the bite every 2 to 3 minutes until you get to the hospital. For flea bites, apply a drop of lavender directly to the bite. For mosquito bites, mix the juice of two lemons or 1 cup cider vinegar with 10 drops lavender and 5 drops thyme, and add to your bath; towel dry and dab lavender directly on the bites.

Thyme—for gnats and midge bites, dilute 3 drops thyme in 1 teaspoon cider vinegar or lemon juice and dab on.

Homeopathy

Ledum—use for insect bites and bee stings relieved by application of cold or ice.

Apis mellifica—for bites with swelling, stinging, or burning pain aggravated by heat.

Staphysagria—if child is hypersensitive to mosquito bites, and the bites become large and irritated.

Herbal Medicine

Aloe vera gel—apply topically; aloe vera contains numerous compounds that facilitate wound healing, including vitamin C, vitamin E, and zinc. Its glycoproteins block inflammatory mediators, thus reducing pain and swelling. Its polysaccharides stimulate epidermal growth and repair.

Echinacea—tincture, taken internally; helps the body heal wounds and stings.

Comfrey—apply gel or use the dried herb, steamed for 5 minutes and wrapped in cheesecloth to make a poultice, to help draw out the poison and relieve the itching.

Supplements

Vitamin C with bioflavonoids—anti-inflammatory, boosts immune response, helps restore cell-wall integrity.

Colds, Cold Sores, Coughs, Fever, Influenza, Sore Throat, Laryngitis

COMMON COLD

Aromatherapy

Common-Cold Bath Blend—add to a hot bath 2 drops thyme, 2 drops tea tree oil, 1 drop eucalyptus, and 3 drops lemon. Inhale deeply.

Common-Cold Inhalation Blend—on a tissue, place 1 drop each thyme, peppermint, eucalyptus, and clove. Inhale deeply every half-hour or so.

Common-Cold Massage Blend—to 1 teaspoon cold-pressed, organic vegetable oil, add 1 drop lemon, 2 drops eucalyptus, and 3 drops rosemary. Use to massage chest, neck, and sinus area (forehead, nose, cheekbones).

Homeopathy

Aconitum—the remedy to use during the first 24 hours when symptoms come on suddenly, especially after exposure to cold. Symptoms may include a dry cough and great thirst.

Allium cepa—for a constant, burning nasal discharge that irritates the nose, a bland tearing from the eyes, and frequent sneezing, all made worse in warm or stuffy rooms.

Arsenicum—for a burning, irritating nasal discharge that is worse on the right side, accompanied by chills, made worse by cold; give if child is restless, weak, and very thirsty but drinks only sips at a time.

Belladonna—for a cold with sudden onset, fever, a flushed red face, glassy eyes, a reddened sore throat.

Euphrasia—if child's eyes tear and burn while the nasal discharge is constant but bland.

Gelsemium—if child has heavy, droopy eyes, weakness and fatigue, chills up and down the spine, and prefers to be alone.

Kali bichromicum—for a cold with thick, stringy nasal discharge, often with pain at the root of the nose.

Pulsatilla—for a stuffy nose with thick yellow discharge; symptoms are worse at night and in stuffy rooms.

Nux vomica—for a runny nose during the day and congestion at night; if symptoms begin after exposure to cold or overeating.

Herbal Medicine

Astragalus—a Chinese herb valued as a tonic that strengthens the body's resistance to disease; clinical studies in China have confirmed that astragalus reduces incidence and shortens duration of the common cold.

Echinacea and goldenseal combination—antiviral echinacea and antibacterial goldenseal both stimulate immune response, and goldenseal helps heal mucus membranes. Echinacea's effects are most potent for the first two or three days; do not use echinacea longer than a week.

Garlic—a natural antibiotic that also helps detoxify the body.

Supplements

Emergen-C—product from Alacer Corporation containing vitamin C, B vitamins, calcium, magnesium, potassium, sodium, manganese, chromium, and zinc; boosts immune function, anti-inflammatory, helps body deal with stress.

Zinc glycine lozenges—zinc is necessary for proper immune function; lozenges containing zinc bound to glycine have been found in studies to have an antiviral effect. Do not give your child a therapeutic dose of zinc (30 milligrams) for more than one week. Normal zinc intake should be 15 milligrams per day.

Beta-carotene—used by the body to produce vitamin A, which heals mucus membranes.

COLD SORES

Aromatherapy

Cold Sore Blend—combine 8 drops geranium, 3 drops lemon, 6 drops chamomile German, 8 drops tea tree oil, and 5 drops lavender. Dip a cotton swab in water, put one drop of the blend on it, and apply to the cold sore once a day.

Homeopathy

Natrum muriaticum—the primary remedy for cold sores, especially for children with dry, cracked lips who get cold sores with other acute infections, such as colds, influenza, sore throat; also, when a cold sore appears after prolonged sun exposure. If the blister contains fluid, it will be clear.

Rhus toxicodendron—for small, inflamed blisters in a cluster, usually with watery, yellow fluid.

Hepar sulphuris—if the cold sore is very sensitive, and the child becomes irritable.

Arsenicum—if the cold sore burns but feels better with warm applications; good for the child who is restless, anxious, fastidious, demanding, chilly, and thirsty (but takes only small sips at a time).

Herbal Medicine

Echinacea and goldenseal combination—both herbs boost immune response; cold sores are caused by the herpes simplex virus, and echinacea is antiviral.

Garlic—studies have shown sulphfur compounds in garlic can destroy herpes simplex.

Goldenseal root—open a capsule, add a few drops of water to make a paste, and apply topically.

Supplements

L-lysine capsules taken internally or L-lysine cream applied topically—an amino acid, lysine fights the herpes virus (another amino acid, arginine, found in high levels in nuts, stimulates the herpes virus, so have your child avoid eating nuts when he has a cold sore).

Selenium—a trace mineral that is both an antioxidant and is essential for proper immune activation.

Emergen-C—product from Alacer Corporation containing vitamin C, B vitamins, calcium, magnesium, potassium, sodium, manganese, chromium, and zinc; boosts immune function, helps body deal with stress.

Folic acid—one of the B vitamins, folic acid helps heal mucus membranes and has been found helpful in healing cold sores.

COUGHS

Aromatherapy

Dry Cough Blend—mix 2 drops eucaplytus, 2 drops lemon, and 2 tablespoons sweetener (for children older than one year old, use honey; if younger, use maple syrup). Dilute 1 teaspoon of this blend in a 4- to 6-ounce glass of warm water, and sip slowly.

Coughs with Mucus Blend—mix 2 drops eucalyptus, 1 drop thyme, and 1 drop tea tree oil with 1 tablespoon sweetener (for children older than 1 year, use honey; if younger, use maple syrup). Add 1 drop of this mixture to a 4- to 6-ounce glass of warm water and sip slowly.

Cough Massage Oil—for either type of cough, combine 3 drops eucalyptus, 2 drops thyme, and 1 tablespoon organic, cold-pressed vegetable oil. Massage into chest and back.

Homeopathy

Aconitum—use during the first 24 hours for a dry cough, especially one that starts after exposure to cold or after a fright.

Spongia—for a dry, barking, or rattling cough aggravated by talking, getting excited, and cold drinks; better after sipping a hot drink.

Bryonia—for a dry, painful cough; even breathing hurts, so the child may put his hands on his chest to lessen movement.

Belladonna—for a cough with high fever and sweating.

Antimonium tartaricum—for a pale, tired child who feels breathless and has a rattling cough due to thick mucus. Do not give if your child has a fever.

Pulsatilla—for the emotional, clingy child with a cough that produces thick yellow or yellow-green expectoration; cough is worse after eating or lying down and is aggravated by being in a warm, stuffy room.

Rumex—for a dry, tickling cough, worse when lying down (especially on the left side) or when breathing cold air.

Coccus cacti—when there is an accumulation of thick, stringy mucus and cold drinks provide short-term relief.

Ipecacuanna—if vomiting, nausea, or nosebleed accompany the cough.

Phosphorus—when chills, laryngitis or hoarseness, or thirst for cold water accompany the cough; aggravated by cold air, talking, lying on the back or left side, strong odors.

Hepar sulphuris—for the later stages of a dry cough with rattling in the chest but difficulty bringing up mucus.

Cough and bronchial syrup (Boericke & Tafel sugar-free)—an excellent homeopathic combination remedy for coughs and congestion.

Herbal Medicine

Licorice root—antibacterial, soothing to throat and respiratory tract as tea or in tincture.

Marshmallow root—given as tea, soothes the throat and respiratory tract.

Mullein tea—helpful in the early stages of a cough, before an expectorant is needed.

Osha root—highly aromatic, helps clear the lungs when cough is productive, good for a dry cough, too.

Slippery elm—in tea or lozenge form, soothes the throat.

Supplements

Emergen-C—product from Alacer Corporation containing vitamin C, B vitamins, calcium, magnesium, potassium, sodium, manganese, chromium, and zinc; boosts immune function, helps body deal with stress.

Calcium and magnesium combination—soothes the nervous system, helps improve circulation, and eases constriction in the lungs.

Zinc glycine lozenges—zinc is necessary for proper immune function; lozenges containing zinc bound to glycine have been found in studies to have an antiviral effect. Do not give your child a therapeutic dose of zinc (30 milligrams) for more than one week. Normal zinc intake should be 15 milligrams per day.

Beta-carotene—used by the body to produce vitamin A, which heals mucus membranes.

FEVER

Aromatherapy

Eucalyptus—cooling, soothing, especially helpful if fever is associated with a cold or other respiratory discomfort. Add 2 or 3 drops to a small bowl of lukewarm water for a sponge bath.

Peppermint—cooling, stimulating, especially helpful if fever is associated with tummy complaint. Add 2 or 3 drops to a small bowl of lukewarm water for a sponge bath.

Lavender—antiseptic, soothing, relaxant, especially helpful if child is anxious and fretful.

Thyme linalol—a powerful antiviral, helps with elimination of toxic wastes from the body; do not use directly on the skin. Add 4 drops to a warm bath.

Homeopathy

Aconitum—for the first 24 hours of a fever, especially one that begins suddenly after exposure to cold.

Anas barbariae (trade name: Oscillococcinum)—for fever associated with the flu.

Arsenicum—if the fever increases between midnight and 2 A.M.; the child is anxious and fidgety.

Belladonna—for sudden fever with chills, a flushed face and body, dilated pupils; worse with noise and light.

Bryonia—if child is irritable, has a strong thirst, wants to be alone, may be constipated.

Gelsemium—if child's whole body feels achy and flushed, eyelids heavy and droopy, has no thirst.

Mercurius solubilis—for a feverish child with offensive-smelling breath, body odor, stool, or urine.

Phosphorus—for a fever accompanied by a cough; the child craves ice cold drinks but may not be able to keep them down.

Herbal Medicine

Echinacea and goldenseal combination—echinacea is antiviral; goldenseal is antibacterial and soothes mucus membranes. Both herbs boost immune response.

Garlic—antibacterial and antiviral.

Ginger tea—promotes perspiration, thus lowering fever.

Supplements

Emergen-C—product from Alacer Corporation containing vitamin C, B vitamins, calcium, magnesium, potassium, sodium, manganese, chromium, and zinc; boosts immune function, anti-inflammatory, helps body deal with stress.

INFLUENZA

Aromatherapy

Eucalyptus—antiviral, anti-inflammatory, analgesic, cools and soothes irritated respiratory passages.

Lavender—antibiotic, antiseptic, sedative, detoxifier, stimulates immune system.

Tea tree—powerful antiseptic, antiviral, antibacterial, antifungal, useful for all sorts of infections.

Thyme linalol—potent antiviral, helps the body eliminate toxic wastes. Use in room air spray, add several drops to a bath, add 1 or 2 drops to 2 tablespoons cold-pressed, organic vegetable oil. Do not apply directly to the skin.

Homeopathy

Anas barbariae (trade name: Oscillococcinum)—the first remedy to give for flu; only effective during the first 48 hours.

Arsenicum—for the child with a red, runny, burning nose who feels worse in a cold room, wants to be left alone, but wants attention every once in a while.

Bryonia—for the child with marked body aches who feels worse with any motion; has a headache in the front part of the head; dry, chapped lips; a dry cough; and a great thirst for cold water.

Gelsemium—for the child with heavy, droopy eyelids, fatigue, aches and chills up and down the spine, weakness, little or no thirst, a headache in the back part of the head.

Eupatorium perfoliatum—for the child who feels a deep aching in muscles and bones, and gets chills, usually in the morning.

Rhus toxicodendron—for the child with muscle aches upon initial movement that feels better with motion. The child is typically restless, especially at night in bed; has a sore throat and is thirsty, but only for sips of water at a time.

Mercurius solubilis—for a lingering flu with a sore throat; bad breath; tender, swollen glands.

Herbal Medicine

Echinacea and goldenseal combination—antiviral echinacea and antibacterial goldenseal both stimulate immune response; goldenseal helps heal mucus membranes. Echinacea's effects are most potent for the first two or three days; do not use echinacea longer than a week.

Goldenseal—its positive effects do not diminish, so it may be used longer than a week if needed.

Supplements

Calcium and magnesium combination—helps ease aches and pains, calming an irritable child and helping to promote sleep.

Vitamin C—necessary for proper immune function, anti-inflammatory.

Zinc picolinate (10 to 15 milligrams) or if sore throat, zinc glycine lozenges—necessary for proper immune function. Lozenges have an antiviral effect; studies have found them especially useful for sore throat.

SORE THROAT, LARYNGITIS

Aromatherapy

Chamomile—antibacterial, antiseptic, anti-inflammatory.

Lavender—antibiotic, relaxant, promotes healing, stimulates immune response.

Thyme—antiviral, antiseptic, helps the body eliminate wastes.

Lemon—antiseptic, antibacterial, tonic.

Sore Throat Blends—for steam inhalations, combine 2 drops chamomile, 3 drops lavender, 1 drop thyme; add to a bowl of hot, steaming water and inhale. For a massage oil, dilute 5 drops chamomile, 1 drop thyme, 2 drops lemon in 1 teaspoon vegetable oil and use to massage neck.

Homeopathy

Aconitum—use during the first 24 hours, especially if the sore throat began suddenly after exposure to cold weather and the child is very thirsty.

Apis mellifica—for red, swollen tonsils; burning, stinging pain relieved by cold drinks, made worse by warmth.

Belladonna—use during the first 48 hours if child has reddened tonsils, burning pain in the throat, flushed red skin, and fever.

Ferrum phosphoricum—if the sore throat is accompanied by fever.

Phosphorus—for a sore throat accompanied by hoarseness, worse in the evening.

Hepar sulphuris—when a sore throat is accompanied by a cough that brings up thick white or yellow mucus, and the child feels better with warm applications on the throat.

Phytolacca—for a dark red throat, swollen glands, much difficulty swallowing.

Lachesis—for a sore throat on the left side, or one that starts on the left and moves to the right, with dark red tonsils and irritability, aggravated by heat.

Lycopodium—for a sore throat on the right side, or one that starts on the right and moves to the left.

Herbal Medicine

Echinacea and goldenseal combination—antiviral echinacea and antibacterial goldenseal both stimulate immune response; goldenseal helps heal mucus membranes. Echinacea's effects are most potent for the first two or three days; do not use echinacea longer than a week.

Licorice root—antibacterial, soothing to throat and respiratory tract as tea or in tincture.

Slippery elm—a demulcent, soothes a sore throat in tea or lozenge form.

Supplements

Emergen-C—product from Alacer Corporation containing vitamin C, B vitamins, calcium, magnesium, potassium, sodium, manganese, chromium, and zinc; boosts immune function, helps body deal with stress.

Calcium and magnesium combination—soothes the nervous system, helps improve circulation, and eases constriction in the lungs.

Zinc glycine lozenges—zinc is necessary for proper immune function; lozenges containing zinc bound to glycine have been found in studies to have an antiviral effect. Do not give your child a therapeutic dose of zinc (30 milligrams) for more than one week. Normal zinc intake should be 15 milligrams per day.

Beta-carotene—used by the body to produce vitamin A, which heals mucus membranes.

Earache

Aromatherapy

Earache Pack 1—Warm 1 teaspoon organic, cold-pressed olive oil. Add 1 drop lavender and 1 drop chamomile. Soak a piece of 100 percent cotton in the mixture and use it to plug the ear gently.

Earache Pack 2—Warm 1 teaspoon organic, cold-pressed olive oil. Add 2 drops lavender, 3 drops tea tree, and 1 drop thyme linalol. Soak a piece of 100 percent cotton in the mixture and use it to plug the ear gently.

Earache Massage Oil—Combine 3 drops chamomile, 1 drop lavender, and 1 drop tea tree oil. Dilute in 1 teaspoon vegetable oil. Gently massage oil around the ear, up the neck, and around the cheekbone, then apply a warm compress to the area.

Homeopathy

Aconitum—use at the onset of an earache when the ear is hot and painful, throbs with pain after exposure to cold, is accompanied by a fever; the child is very thirsty and also may have a dry cough.

Allium cepa—for an earache accompanied by a cold with a burning, watery, acrid nasal discharge.

Belladonna—for a throbbing earache accompanied by fever, red face, dilated pupils, hot and moist skin; the earache comes on suddenly and may be accompanied by swollen glands; the child may be agitated. Generally used during the first three days of an earache.

Calcarea carbonica—for the child with a throbbing earache with a thick, yellow, offensive-smelling discharge; the child is normally chilly yet has a hot, sweaty head; sweat and stools smell sour; the child also may be constipated.

Chamomilla—for the child who is in great discomfort and irritable; who demands things, then refuses them when offered; whose pains are made worse by cold; whose ears feel stuffed up.

Ferrum phosphoricum—for an earache with a fever, usually on the left side; symptoms have slower onset and are less intense than the earaches that respond to aconitum and belladonna.

Pulsatilla—for an earache that comes on gradually, often with or after a cold, and that is aggravated by heat, lessened with cold applications, fresh air.

Mercurius dulcis—for long-lasting or chronic ear infections or for acute infections with pus and a gluey, burning, offensive-smelling discharge that is worse at night and from warmth.

Herbal Medicine

Echinacea and goldenseal combination—echinacea is antiviral; goldenseal is antibacterial and soothes mucus membranes. Both herbs stimulate immune function.

Garlic—antibacterial and antiviral.

Mullein oil—a traditional Native American herbal remedy; put 1 or 2 drops of gently heated mullein oil in the affected ear to soothe and reduce swelling and inflammation.

Supplements

Probiotics—friendly flora that help maintain a healthy digestive tract, especially needed if your child has been given antibiotics, which destroy not just the bad bacteria but the necessary, health-promoting ones, too.

FOS—fructooligosaccharides, the favorite food of probiotics.

Emergen-C—product from Alacer Corporation containing vitamin C, B vitamins, calcium, magnesium, potassium, sodium, manganese, chromium, and zinc; boosts immune function, helps body deal with stress.

Calcium and magnesium combination—soothes the nervous system, helps improve circulation.

Zinc glycine lozenges—zinc is necessary for proper immune function; lozenges containing zinc bound to glycine have been found in studies to have an antiviral effect. Do not give your child a therapeutic dose of zinc (30 milligrams) for more than one week. Normal zinc intake should be 15 milligrams per day.

Beta-carotene—used by the body to produce vitamin A, which heals mucus membranes.

Eye Problems: Conjunctivitis, Styes

CONJUNCTIVITIS

Aromatherapy

Conjunctivitis Blend—mix 1 drop chamomile, 1 drop witch hazel, and 2 tablespoons rosewater; leave for 7 hours, strain through a paper coffee filter, and apply as a compress on closed eyelids.

Homeopathy

Euphrasia—if eyes are burning, itching, tearing.

Pulsatilla—if eyes produce a thick, yellowish discharge that makes eyelids feel "glued" together upon waking.

Herbal Medicine

Echinacea and goldenseal combination—echinacea fights viral infections; goldenseal fights bacteria and soothes mucus membranes.

Eyebright—make a tea to use in a warm compress.

Goldenseal root powder—use to make a warm compress.

Supplements

Emergen-C—product from Alacer Corporation containing vitamin C, B vitamins, calcium, magnesium, potassium, sodium, manganese, chromium, and zinc; boosts immune function, helps body deal with stress.

Quercetin plus other bioflavonoids—anti-inflammatory, antiallergenic, works with vitamin C to boost immune function.

Beta-carotene—used by the body to produce vitamin A, heals mucus membranes, important for immune function, adrenal function, healthy eyes.

Zinc picolinate—a well-absorbed form of zinc; zinc is essential for proper immune function; therapeutic dosage of zinc at 15 to 20 milligrams twice daily for up to one week. (Normal zinc intake should be 15 milligrams per day.)

STYES

Aromatherapy

Stye treatment—boil 2 teaspoons rosewater, add 1 drop chamomile, strain through a paper coffee filter. Place 1 drop of neat (undiluted) lavender on a cotton ball and dab on the cheekbone under the stye, keeping the eye closed. Soak a pad in the chamomile-rosewater solution. Apply to closed eyelid as a compress. Repeat twice daily.

Homeopathy

Aconite—as soon as you notice a stye developing.

Pulsatilla—for almost painless styes, usually appearing on the upper lid.

Hepar sulphuris—for painful, hypersensitive styes aggravated by cold.

Apis—for a stye with swelling, burning, stinging pains relieved by cold.

Herbal Medicine

Eyebright—relieves redness and swelling.

Goldenseal—fights bacteria, boosts immune response, soothes mucus membranes.

Supplements

Beta-carotene—converted in the body to vitamin A, which helps heal eyes, soothe mucus membranes.

Emergen-C—product from Alacer Corporation containing vitamin C, B vitamins, calcium, magnesium, potassium, sodium, manganese, chromium, and zinc; boosts immune function, helps body deal with stress.

Zinc picolinate—a well-absorbed form of zinc; zinc is essential for proper immune function; therapeutic dose 15 to 20 milligrams twice daily for up to one week. Normal zinc intake should be 15 milligrams per day.

Head Lice

Aromatherapy

Tea Tree Oil Solution—add 25 drops tea tree to 1 pint water and rub into your child's scalp and hair three times daily.

Therapeutic Head Lice Blend—combine 20 drops chamomile German, 10 drops lavender, and 5 drops lemon. Dilute in 2 tablespoons organic, cold-pressed olive oil. Massage into the scalp, leave on overnight, and shampoo out the following morning. After shampooing, use the following hair rinse.

Lice Deterrent Hair Rinse—combine 5 drops rosemary, 5 drops geranium, 5 drops lavender, 5 drops eucalyptus, and 5 drops lemon. Add 2 drops of this blend to the final rinse after shampooing.

Homeopathy

Sulphur—a good remedy for heated, inflamed skin conditions, including lice.

Herbal Medicine

Echinacea and goldenseal combination—echinacea is antiviral; goldenseal is antibacterial; both stimulate immune function and will help prevent a secondary infection.

Garlic—antifungal, antiparasitic, immune-enhancing properties.

Balsam of Peru—antiparasitic, destroys the mite *Acarus* and its eggs, and is useful against a variety of skin conditions. Apply to the scalp, then comb your child's hair with a fine-tooth comb to remove lice and eggs. Don't take internally.

Supplements

Emergen-C—product from Alacer Corporation containing vitamin C, B vitamins, calcium, magnesium, potassium, sodium, manganese, chromium, and zinc; boosts immune function, helps body deal with stress.

Quercetin plus other bioflavonoids—anti-inflammatory, antiallergenic, works with vitamin C to boost immune function.

Beta-carotene—used by the body to produce vitamin A, heals mucus membranes, important for immune function.

Zinc picolinate—a well-absorbed form of zinc; zinc is essential for proper immune function; therapeutic dose 15 to 20 milligrams twice daily for up to one week. Normal zinc intake should be 15 milligrams per day.

Sleep Problems: Bedwetting, Insomnia

BEDWETTING

Aromatherapy

Chamomile Roman—diuretic, sedative, calming.

Geranium—soothes the emotions, a nerve tonic.

Lavender—a mood tonic, circulatory stimulant.

No More Bedwetting Blend—use 6 drops of any one of the above oils (or combine 2 drops of each) and dilute in 2 tablespoons cold-pressed, organic vegetable oil. Massage your child's feet and lower back before reading his bedtime story. Right before going to sleep, have your child make one last trip to the bathroom.

Homeopathy

Calcarea phosphorica—for the restless child who voids small amounts but doesn't wake up.

Causticum—for the child who wets the bed right after falling asleep; often this child has a pale face with dark circles under the eyes.

Lycopodium—for the intelligent, sensitive child who often acts older than he is, soaks the bed late at night, and is terribly embarrassed by it.

Equisetum—for the child who often has nightmares that wake her; whose bedwetting is heavy and frequent.

Pulsatilla—for the sensitive child, often fair-haired, who feels the urge to urinate so strongly that she cannot make it to the bathroom quickly enough.

Sepia—for the child who wets the bed during the first two hours of sleep.

Herbal Medicine

Chamomile tea—soothing, relaxing, relieves anxiety.

Supplements

Calcium and magnesium combination—calcium and magnesium relax muscles, improve blood flow, soothe a keyed-up or stressed nervous system.

INSOMNIA

Aromatherapy

Chamomile Roman—sedative, calming.

Lavender—sedative, relaxant.

Geranium—soothes the emotions, a nerve tonic.

Better Sleep Bath—add 6 drops of any one of the above oils or a combination to a very warm before-bedtime bath.

Better Sleep Blend—use 10 drops of any one of the above oils or a combination diluted in 3 tablespoons cold-pressed, organic vegetable oil. Massage your child's feet and back at bedtime.

Homeopathy

Carbo vegetalis—for the child who wakes up with a stomachache.

Coffea cruda—homeopathic coffee. This remedy helps relax the excited child who can't wind down mentally or physically and is full of plans for the next day.

Ignatia—for the child who yawns and sighs frequently or who has had a recent saddening experience.

Kali phosphoricum—for the child who wakes from a nightmare, is very anxious, and cannot fall back to sleep.

Nux vomica—for insomnia caused by mental strain, excessive study.

Arsenicum—for the anxious child who has scary dreams, is chilly and thirsty, but only takes small sips at a time.

Chamomilla—for the child who is irritable or in pain; demands things but then refuses them when offered; is sleepy but cannot fall asleep or, if he does manage to fall asleep, moans and twitches.

Pulsatilla—for the child who doesn't want to go to bed because she doesn't want to leave her parents; who wants a light on in her room; who dislikes covers but wakes up cold when she kicks them off.

Rhus toxicdendron—uncomfortable and restless, this child tosses and turns, wakes up feeling stiff, but feels better as he moves around.

Staphysagria—for the child who is upset, brooding on past events, has frightful dreams, may have been abused.

Herbal Medicine

Chamomile—a gentle relaxant, safe even for children as young as two; give as a warm tea before bedtime.

Passionflower—a gentle relaxant, safe for children over four years old; give as a warm tea before bedtime.

Skullcap—an effective relaxant, safe for children over six years old; give as a warm tea or in tincture or capsule form before bedtime.

Valerian—safe for children over twelve years old; give in capsule, tea, or tincture before bedtime.

Supplements

Brewer's yeast—high in B vitamins and minerals that soothe and balance the nervous system.

Calcium and magnesium combination—calcium and magnesium relax muscles, improve blood flow, soothe a keyed-up or stressed nervous system.

Sunburn

Aromatherapy

Lavender—apply a cold water compress, then 2 drops of neat (undiluted) lavender directly on any especially sunburned areas. Alternately, add 10 drops lavender to a tepid bath and soak for at least 10 minutes. Gently blot dry and apply aloe vera gel or chamomile lotion.

Homeopathy

Urtica urens—homeopathic stinging nettle that quickly reduces the stinging, burning pain.

Ferrum phosphoricum—if your child develops a slight fever.

Herbal Medicine

Aloe vera gel—aloe vera contains numerous compounds that heal sun-burned skin, including vitamin C, vitamin E, and zinc. Other compounds block inflammatory mediators, thus reducing pain and swelling. Store 100 percent aloe vera gel in the refrigerator for extra soothing, cooling relief.

Comfrey—use dried herb to make tea, or use in gel form; comfrey contains allantoin, an anti-inflammatory compound that promotes healing.

Supplements

Beta-carotene—converted in the body to vitamin A, necessary for healthy skin, promotes healing.

Emergen-C—product from Alacer Corporation containing vitamin C, B vitamins, calcium, magnesium, potassium, sodium, manganese, chromium, and zinc; boosts immune function, helps body deal with stress, aids in healing.

Zinc picolinate—a well-absorbed form of zinc; zinc is essential for proper immune function; therapeutic dose 15 to 20 milligrams twice daily for up to one week. Normal zinc intake should be 15 milligrams per day.

Tummy Troubles: Constipation, Diarrhea, Gas-Indigestion-Nausea

CONSTIPATION

Aromatherapy

Geranium—antiseptic and astringent with a delightful and relaxing fragrance.

Rosemary—a gentle muscular stimulant.

Combination formula—blend 4 drops each geranium and rosemary in 2 tablespoons cold-pressed, organic vegetable oil and massage tummy and back in clockwise movement. Give your child a tall glass of half-fruit juice, half-water first.

Homeopathy

Alumina—for the child with small, hard, dry pelletlike stools that may be covered with mucus.

Bryonia alba—for the child with large, hard, dry stools; a white-coated tongue, a craving for cold drinks; whose symptoms are aggravated by warmth, and who feels better in open-air, cool rooms.

Calcarea carbonica—for the child who smells sour, has sour-smelling stools, may dislike milk or be allergic to it, may feel better when constipated.

Lycopodium—if the child experiences pain right before a bowel movement.

Natrum muriaticum—for the child who craves salt, is thirsty, yet has hard, dry stools.

Nux vomica—for the child who keeps feeling as if he has to defecate but can't; whose constipation begins after overindulging and may be accompanied by heartburn, bloating, gas, headache.

Herbal Medicine

Aloe vera juice—combine 1 tablespoon food-grade, liquid aloe vera juice with fruit juice or applesauce. Give twice daily.

Slippery elm—a demulcent, slippery elm soothes intestinal walls and provides mucilage to ease out stools.

Licorice—tea or tincture is soothing to irritated intestinal walls.

Supplements

Flaxseed oil—add 1 to 10 drops to your child's oatmeal or smoothie twice daily.

Flaxseed meal—provides bulk and anti-inflammatory omega-3 oil.

Probiotics—friendly flora that help maintain a healthy digestive tract.

FOS—fructooligosaccharides, the favorite food of probiotics.

DIARRHEA

Aromatherapy

Food-related Diarrhea Massage Oil Formula—Combine 2 drops chamomile, 3 drops peppermint, and 1 drop eucalyptus. Dilute in 1 teaspoon cold-pressed, organic vegetable oil and massage into tummy.

Nervous agitation–related Diarrhea Massage Oil Formula—Combine 1 drop chamomile, 2 drops eucalyptus, and 3 drops lavender. Dilute in 1 teaspoon cold-pressed, organic vegetable oil and massage into tummy.

Viral-related Diarrhea Massage Oil Formula—Combine 3 drops thyme, 2 drops lavender, and 1 drop tea tree. Dilute in 1 teaspoon cold-pressed, organic vegetable oil and massage into tummy.

Homeopathy

Arsenicum—for diarrhea related to food poisoning, anxiety, or stress.

Calcarea carbonica—for diarrhea after eating dairy products.

China—for diarrhea after eating too much fruit.

Argentum nitricum—for diarrhea after eating too much sugar.

Pulsatilla—for diarrhea after eating too much fatty food.

Natrum muriaticum—for recurrent diarrhea; for the child who craves salt.

Mercurius solubis—for green, foul-smelling diarrhea.

Colocynthis—helps alleviate the twisting, cramping pains that often accompany diarrhea.

Magnesia phosphorica—helps relax the bowel and ease cramping.

Herbal Medicine

Carob—tastes like chocolate, helps to settle the intestines and stop diarrhea; mix with water and drink.

Goldenseal—antibacterial, soothes mucus membranes.

Slippery elm—powdered slippery elm bark helps heal and soothe distressed intestines; add 1 teaspoon powder to juice or applesauce two or three times daily.

Supplements

Probiotics—friendly flora that help maintain a healthy digestive tract.

FOS—fructooligosaccharides, the favorite food of probiotics.

Omega-3 essential fatty acids—salmon or flaxseed oil are good sources of these anti-inflammatory essential fats, needed for healthy intestinal mucosa.

GAS, INDIGESTION, NAUSEA

Aromatherapy

Dill and Geranium Tummyache Massage Formula—dilute 9 drops dill and 6 drops geranium in 2 tablespoons cold-pressed, organic vegetable oil. Massage into tummy and back in a clockwise direction.

Peppermint—an excellent carminative; blend 15 drops peppermint in 2 tablespoons vegetable oil and massage into tummy and back in clockwise direction.

Homeopathy

Arsenicum—for burning pains in the stomach or rectum accompanied by chills. Child may be thirsty, but takes only a few sips at a time.

Bryonia alba—for digestive discomfort after motion, with thirst for cold liquids, and nausea on sitting up.

Pulsatilla—for indigestion after eating fatty foods such as ice cream or fried food; for the child who is aggravated by stuffy rooms but feels better with open air, attention, sympathy.

Nux vomica—for indigestion after overeating or mental stress; the remedy for a food hangover.

Herbal Medicine

Chamomile—serve as a tea to help calm a sick, restless child.

Ginger—a gastrointestinal tonic, ginger tones the intestinal wall and prevents spasms, thus alleviating nausea, vomiting, and accompanying stomachache.

Peppermint—a carminative, promotes the elimination of intestinal gas.

Supplements

Activated charcoal capsules—absorbs toxins and gas.

Probiotics—friendly flora that help maintain a healthy digestive tract.

FOS—fructooligosaccharides, the favorite food of probiotics.

Flaxseed meal—a good source of soothing fiber and anti-inflammatory essential fatty acids.

Omega-3 essential fatty acids—salmon or flaxseed oil are the best sources of these essential fats that are anti-inflammatory and promote the health of intestinal mucosa.

Childhood Viral Infections: Chickenpox, Measles, Rubella (German Measles), Mumps

CHICKENPOX

Aromatherapy

Itch Be Gone Lotion—add 10 drops lavender and 10 drops chamomile German to a 4-ounce bottle of calamine lotion. Shake well and apply all over the body twice a day.

Itch Be Gone Spray—add 10 drops tea tree to 1 pint of water and use as an antiviral air spray.

Itch Be Gone Bath—add 2 drops lavender to 1 cup of bicarbonate of soda and add to the bath.

Homeopathy

Aconitum—use during the initial onset when the rash is accompanied by fever, restlessness, increased thirst.

Antimonium crudum—if the child's tongue is coated white and if pustules itch after a bath or exposure to water or warmth.

Apis mellifica—if the rash stings and feels worse with warmth, better with cold.

Belladonna—if the rash is accompanied by a severe headache, flushed face, hot skin, and drowsiness, yet child is unable to fall asleep.

Rhus toxicodendron—homeopathic poison ivy, this is the most common remedy for chickenpox; for the restless child with intense itching, especially at night and from scratching.

Herbal Medicine

Burdock root—high in trace minerals, burdock root helps detoxify the body and heal skin lesions.

Red clover—like burdock, high in trace minerals, helps detoxify the body and heal skin lesions.

Echinacea and goldenseal combination—echinacea is antiviral; goldenseal is antibacterial and soothes mucus membranes. Both herbs stimulate immune function.

Chamomile tea—helps calm a restless child.

Supplements

Emergen-C—product from Alacer Corporation containing vitamin C, B vitamins, calcium, magnesium, potassium, sodium, manganese, chromium, and zinc; boosts immune function, helps body deal with stress.

Quercetin plus other bioflavonoids—anti-inflammatory, antiallergenic, works with vitamin C to boost immune function.

Beta-carotene—used by the body to produce vitamin A, heals mucus membranes, important for immune function.

Zinc picolinate—a well-absorbed form of zinc; zinc is essential for proper immune function; therapeutic dose 15 to 20 milligrams twice daily for up to one week. Normal zinc intake should be 15 milligrams per day.

Calcium and magnesium combination—soothes the nervous system, helps relax your child.

MEASLES

Aromatherapy

Measles Wash Solution—combine 3 drops chamomile German and 3 drops lavender. Add to 1 pint tepid water and use to gently sponge down the child. Then add 5 drops each chamomile German and lavender to a 4-ounce bottle of calamine lotion, shake well, and use to cover the spots.

Homeopathy

Aconitum—for the first stage of measles with sudden onset of fever, skin rash, nasal discharge, reddened eyes, dry cough, restless sleep.

Euphrasia—if, along with the rash, the child has bland nasal discharge and frequent burning tears that irritate the cheeks.

Gelsemium—for the feverish child with droopy eyelids and a croupy cough; the child may complain of feeling tired and chilly, have aching muscles, a headache and/or a runny nose.

Pulsatilla—for later stages of measles if the child is clingy, has a yellow or greenish nasal discharge, and feels worse in stuffy rooms but better with an open window and fresh air.

Sulphur—if the rash is aggravated by heat, the child's eyelids are inflamed, and the eyes burn.

Herbal Medicine

Echinacea and goldenseal combination—echinacea is antiviral; goldenseal is antibacterial and soothes mucus membranes. Both herbs stimulate immune function.

Garlic—antibacterial and antiviral.

Shiitake mushroom—stimulates immune response. Cook and add to soup or give in capsule form.

Chamomile tea—calms a restless child.

Ginger tea—can help decrease chills and increase perspiration, thus bringing down a fever. Be sure your child is tucked under the covers after drinking the tea. If she perspires heavily, be prepared to change her out of her wet bedclothes and into dry ones.

Supplements

Emergen-C—product from Alacer Corporation containing vitamin C, B vitamins, calcium, magnesium, potassium, sodium, manganese, chromium, and zinc; boosts immune function, helps body deal with stress.

Quercetin plus other bioflavonoids—anti-inflammatory, antiallergenic, works with vitamin C to boost immune function.

Beta-carotene—used by the body to produce vitamin A, heals mucus membranes, important for immune function.

Zinc picolinate—a well-absorbed form of zinc; zinc is essential for proper immune function; therapeutic dose 15 to 20 milligrams twice daily for up to one week. Normal zinc intake should be 15 milligrams per day.

RUBELLA (GERMAN MEASLES)

Aromatherapy

Rubella Away Spray—add 10 drops tea tree to 1 pint water and use as an antiviral air spray.

Rubella Wash Solution—combine 15 drops chamomile Roman, 15 drops lavender, and 5 drops tea tree. Add 4 drops of this blend to a pint of warm water and use to sponge down the child once a day.

Homeopathy

Ferrum phosphoricum—administer during the first 24 hours if there is fever.

Natrum muriaticum—if the rash is accompanied by oral canker sores, swollen glands, and sore throat.

Phytolacca—if the rash is accompanied by eye pain, swollen glands, and a sore throat, and is relieved by cold drinks.

Pulsatilla—if the rash is accompanied by a stuffy nose with mucus discharge, and the child is clingy and weepy.

Herbal Medicine

Echinacea and goldenseal combination—echinacea is antiviral; goldenseal is antibacterial and soothes mucus membranes. Both herbs stimulate immune function.

Garlic—antibacterial and antiviral.

Licorice root—antibacterial, soothing to the throat and respiratory tract as tea or in tincture.

Chamomile tea—helps calm a restless child.

Supplements

Emergen-C—product from Alacer Corporation containing vitamin C, B vitamins, calcium, magnesium, potassium, sodium, manganese, chromium, and zinc; boosts immune function, helps body deal with stress.

Quercetin plus other bioflavonoids—anti-inflammatory, antiallergenic, works with vitamin C to boost immune function.

Beta-carotene—used by the body to produce vitamin A, heals mucus membranes, important for immune function.

Zinc picolinate—a well-absorbed form of zinc; zinc is essential for proper immune function; therapeutic dose 15 to 20 milligrams twice daily for up to one week. Normal zinc intake should be 15 milligrams per day.

MUMPS

Aromatherapy

Mumps Away Air Spray—to 2½ cups water, add 5 drops tea tree or lavender or a combination. Fill a clean spray bottle and spray in the child's bedroom so she will inhale the essential oil molecules in the moistened air.

Mumps Massage Oil Blend—Combine 10 drops each tea tree, lavender, coriander, and lemon. Add 30 drops of this blend to 2 tablespoons vegetable oil and apply gently around the sore area, the back of the neck, and the tummy. Combine the remaining 10 drops with a pint of water and use as an antiviral air spray.

Homeopathy

Belladonna—for the first stage of a mumps infection, especially when the illness begins suddenly and the child has a reddened face and swollen, hot throat glands.

Bryonia—for the child whose right gland is more swollen than the left, and who may be constipated.

Rhus toxicodendron—for a child whose left gland is more swollen than the right, and who feels stiff and achy in the morning but somewhat better as he continues to move.

Mercurius—for the second stage of mumps infection; for the child with swollen glands, a sore throat, bad taste in the mouth, bad breath, and increased salivation. A boy may have swollen testicles.

Phytolacca—for the child whose salivary glands are firm and hard, and who has shooting pains in the ear when swallowing.

Pulsatilla—for the second stage of mumps infection when the child feels worse in stuffy rooms, better in cool air, has little thirst, and has physical and emotional symptoms that constantly change.

Herbal Medicine

Echinacea and goldenseal combination—echinacea is antiviral; goldenseal is antibacterial and soothes mucus membranes. Both herbs stimulate immune function.

Garlic—antibacterial and antiviral.

Shiitake mushroom—stimulates immune response. Cook and add to soup or give in capsule form.

Chamomile tea—calms a restless child.

Supplements

Emergen-C—product from Alacer Corporation containing vitamin C, B vitamins, calcium, magnesium, potassium, sodium, manganese, chromium, and zinc; boosts immune function, helps body deal with stress.

Quercetin plus other bioflavonoids—anti-inflammatory, antiallergenic, works with vitamin C to boost immune function.

Beta-carotene—used by the body to produce vitamin A, heals mucus membranes, important for proper immune function.

Zinc glycine lozenges—zinc is necessary for proper immune function; lozenges containing zinc bound to glycine have been found in studies to have an antiviral effect. Do not give your child a therapeutic dose of zinc (30 milligrams) for more than one week. Normal zinc intake should be 15 milligrams per day.

Warts

Aromatherapy

Wart No More Blend—to 2 teaspoons cider vinegar, add 10 drops lemon and 5 drops cypress. Shake well. Using a cotton swab, apply twice daily to the wart only, avoiding the surrounding skin.

Homeopathy

Thuja—for all warts, except plantar warts. Use twice daily.

Ruta—for plantar warts, especially on the palm of the hand.

Causticum—for flat warts, most often on the fingers, which bleed easily and may be inflamed and painful.

Nitric acid—for large, jagged warts that itch, sting, and bleed when washed.

Antimonium crudum—for hard, smooth warts; for the child who overeats, has a white-coated tongue, and has digestive complaints.

Herbal Medicine

Garlic—antibacterial, antiviral, antifungal, immune-enhancing.

Shiitake mushroom—has immune-stimulating and antiviral effects.

Supplements

Beta-carotene—converted in the body to vitamin A, necessary for healthy skin and mucosa.

Emergen-C—product from Alacer Corporation containing vitamin C, B vitamins, calcium, magnesium, potassium, sodium, manganese, chromium, and zinc; boosts immune function, helps body deal with stress.

Zinc picolinate—a well-absorbed form of zinc; zinc is essential for proper immune function; therapeutic dose 15 to 20 milligrams twice daily for up to one week. Normal zinc intake should be 15 milligrams per day.

PART 3

COMPLEMENTARY THERAPIES

Chapter 10

Herbal Medicine

Plant-based remedies such as ginger to treat upset stomach and echinacea to treat cold and flu are centuries-old traditions. Herbal medicine is one of the world's oldest healing models, dating back 5,000 years to China, and centuries in the West among Native Americans.

Herbal remedies are generally safe, effective, and inexpensive alternatives to high-cost synthetic drugs. According to Rob McCaleb, president of the Herb Research Foundation in Boulder, Colorado, clinical studies show that garlic reduces blood pressure, licorice root heals ulcers of the small intestines, and echinacea boosts the immune system. In addition, herbs provide benefits unavailable in human-made drugs. "For example, modern medicine has no synthetic drug that can save the lives of liver-poisoning victims like the herb milk thistle does. Western medicine has no immune-system stimulant such as the herb echinacea," McCaleb points out.

Herbal medicine is a consumer-driven revolution, says James Duke, Ph.D., one of America's foremost authorities on medicinal plants and herbs, and author of *The Green Pharmacy*. Pharmaceutical drugs are responsible for approximately 150,000 American deaths per year, he notes. "Three out of every 1,000 people who go to the hospital are killed by the pharmaceuticals they're given. This is obviously causing Americans to look to alternatives such as herbs."

Indeed, a recent study in the *Journal of the American Medical Association* reported that 3 out of every 1,000 hospital patients are killed by pharmaceuticals each year. While herbal medicine is widely accepted in other parts of the world, Duke believes that the introduction of antibiotics in the 1940s caused the demise of herbal medicine in this country: "At first, everyone was so excited about antibiotics because they worked so well. Now we know that antibiotics have created superbacteria, and the antibiotics aren't working so well anymore. We have to go back to herbal medicine." Herbal medicine is more in tune with our bodies' own healing abilities than are pharmaceutical drugs, he adds.

AN HERBAL PHARMACY

Numerous herbs can help you with every childhood illness. The materia medica at the back of this book (see Appendix A) explains many of them to you. I advise parents to work with a health care practitioner who is familiar with herbal medicine. Herbs are very potent, and children do not need much of them to get an effect. It's best to work with a trained practitioner.

Following are the five herbs that I've found most useful and effective.

1. *Peppermint.* When a child has gas or an upset stomach, the first strategy is to brew a strong pot of peppermint tea to which honey is added. A child accepts this eagerly. If a child is vomiting, concentrated peppermint tea poured over crushed ice is the first thing to offer when the child is ready for liquids. An herbal tincture called Minty Ginger, made by Herbs for Kids, can be administered by dropper when there's no time to make tea. Chilled peppermint/chamomile tea is helpful for reducing fever. A washcloth dipped into this lukewarm tea can be rubbed across the child's head, legs, and feet to bring down the fever.

2. *Ginger.* For an upset stomach or for cold and flu, I use liquid ginger tincture, which I drop into a glass of water. (My favorite brand is HerbPharm.) I suggest tasting it first because it may need to be sweetened with either honey or white grape juice. Ginger is a very warming herb. I also use the herbal tincture Minty Ginger in this situation. Ginger is my personal favorite herb for many different conditions, such as prevention of motion sickness and relief of migraine headaches.

3. *Echinacea.* Some children like the taste of echinacea in liquid tincture, which should be administered by the dropperful at the onset of a cold or flu. Give it to the child for two or three days and then stop. Studies

show that this herb is effective only for a few days at a time; however, it can boost the immune system and help the body fight an infection. Many children also like the taste of a chewable echinacea tablet called Esberitox, made by Phyto Pharmica.

4. *Garlic.* I recommend giving your child one oder-free garlic tablet every day. The ones made by Kwai are small and easy to swallow. Garlic has so many benefits ranging from cancer prevention to heart health to immune strengthening.

5. *Elder/Yarrow/Peppermint blend.* This formula made by Herbs for Kids is the first thing I reach for when my daughter gets a fever. These three herbs in combination can help bring down a fever naturally, and they offer many other benefits from calming the stomach to treating cold and flu.

HOW AND WHY YOU SHOULD USE HERBAL MEDICINE

James Duke has spent thirty years working as a botanist for the U.S. Department of Agriculture, specializing in medicinal plants, and he has studied healing herbs all over the world, including China and the Amazon. In his best-selling book *The Green Pharmacy,* Duke evaluates the herbal medicines used around the world for 120 diseases from arthritis to migraines, rating them in terms of their effectiveness. I had the opportunity to interview him and would like to share his insights with you.

Q: *You were interested in herbs long before they became popular with the general public. What do you think is causing this sudden surge in popularity?*

Duke: Herbs are popular now because we're tired of the harmful side effects of medicines. Pharmaceuticals will kill nearly 150,000 Americans a year.

Herbs are user-friendly. People are getting good results from herbs without harmful side effects. The good news is spreading fast about herbs, through word-of-mouth, from herbalists and New Agers to the general public.

Q: *Why should someone who has never tried herbs before try them now?*

Duke: Pharmaceuticals may be the answer for you if you *have* been diagnosed with Lyme disease, though it's often misdiagnosed; if you *are* getting to talk to your doctor; if you *can* afford his prescription; and if you're *not* deficient in any minerals or vitamins. If you satisfy all those requirements, the silver bullet approach of pharmaceuticals may help you. If not, the herb, which is a potpourri of many useful components, will more likely help you.

The medical world is realizing they were wrong twenty years ago when they told us that no one was deficient in vitamins or minerals. The quack busters told us that vitamins just made expensive urine. Now, hardly a day goes by when we don't learn that many of us are deficient in one or another vitamin or mineral. All herbs contain hundreds of useful compounds, from minerals to vitamins to as-yet-unidentified substances. Herbs contain not one but many natural chemicals that might prevent, alleviate, or cure most of our diseases.

Critics of herbal medicine say that few or none of them have been proven safe and effective in the half-billion-dollar studies required to meet the FDA standards for a new, approved drug. Well, that's almost true. Herb companies, unlike pharmaceutical firms, do not have that kind of money to prove what empirical common sense tells them and told their ancestors—that herbs work! Who wants to spend half a billion dollars to prove the safety and effectiveness of an herb that your grandmother took to relieve her migraines? How would the herb companies make their money back? If they paid the $500 million for an FDA-approved drug for feverfew, you and I could still grow it in our backyard and self-medicate.

Q: *But many people think, "If I have an upset stomach, I want to reach for something that I know will work because I've tried it before—like Pepto-Bismol." It's frightening for some people to try an herbal medicine when they need relief from some type of discomfort. Why shouldn't they just keep using the pharmaceuticals?*

Duke: Your genes have been exposed to the natural compounds in plants for thousands of years, and your genes have not been exposed to synthetic over-the-counter drugs. This is why we're having problems with synthetics causing so many side effects. In one ten-year period, over half

of the newly FDA-approved drugs had to be recalled due to unantici-
pated side effects—problems that did not surface in these half-billion-
dollar studies. You know it takes twelve years and $500 million to get a
new FDA-approved drug. But all the side effects don't even surface during the trials.

Your body and my body have never messed with these synthetic
compounds before. However, we *have* been exposed to the natural substances in plants for millions of years. My DNA, RNA, my genes, and
my immune system have already experienced most or all of the natural
phytochemicals that my ancestors ingested. My genes and immune system know nothing of tomorrow's new synthetic compounds. Given the
choice between an herbal alternative and a pharmaceutical, I'll most
often take the herbal alternative myself, because it's usually cheaper,
more environmentally friendly, gentler on the body, and often as effective, and almost always safer than the pharmaceutical.

Q: *Let's say I decide to try herbal medicine for the first time and walk into a natural*
foods store looking for a remedy. Where do I start? It's a little overwhelming. What
advice do you have for first-time herbal buyers?

Duke: That's the toughest question I ever tried to answer. When you
walk into an herb shop with no background in herbal medicine, you're
at the mercy of the retailers and the labels on the herb products. You've
got to put some tough questions to the retailers. Ask them if they would
take the herb you're about to buy. Make them tell you why.

If you're a novice, it's better to start with a better-known herb such
as echinacea and a better-known brand. The manufacturer's reputation
is important in determining quality. If the retailer can't answer all of your
questions, call the manufacturer. Ask about product testing, handling, and
pricing. Does the manufacturer have adequate laboratory and testing
facilities to ensure proper herb identification, purity of raw materials and
finished products, and potency verification? Is the manufacturer in the
business for slow, reliable growth or for a quick profit?

Read the labels carefully. Are fillers used? Is the product the right plant
and the right plant part? Are there warnings or a list of counterindica-
tions? Compare dosages. Sometimes the cheapest product requires 2 or 3
capsules to equal 1 capsule of another brand. Compare prices. If one

brand is substantially less than other brands, it is often, though not always, a good indication that quality has been compromised.

And I recommend standardized herbs to beginners. I personally never take a standardized herb, except when I'm on the road. But a naive consumer is at the mercy of the label, the brand, and the retailer. If they take a standardized herb, at least there's a good chance it will have the desired effect. And if a first-time herb user doesn't get the desired effect the first time they try herbs, they'll never try them again.

Also, before you go into an herb store, you should know what's ailing you, and you should use herbal reference books. Of course, I like to recommend my book *The Green Pharmacy*. It's user-friendly.

Q: *I think it's easy for a beginner to be confused by the different forms of herbal medicine from liquid tinctures and powdered capsules to teas. What's your preference?*

Duke: At home, I prefer fresh herbs. On the road, I want standardized extracts because they're fast and convenient. In most cases, a standardized capsule is better than a tincture. Michael Murray, N.D., says it costs twenty times more to get hypericin from tincture of St. John's wort than from a standardized capsule.

The bin herbs that you find in the mom-and-pop herb shops are not very reliable. Every time you smell the herb, it has lost a chemical. An herb in a bin is constantly changing, creating an infinitely different profile with the more volatile components leaving fastest. Volatiles are readily lost in bulk herbs. For highly aromatic herbs, you're better off with a tincture or alcohol extract. With other herbs, you're better off with standardized capsules. With some herbs, I take both forms for different reasons, like echinacea. I take both the capsule and tincture of echinacea. The capsules contain more of some active ingredients than the tinctures and vice versa.

The best thing about herbs is the great variety of useful compounds they contain, and the worst thing about herbs is the wide fluctuation in the quantities of useful compounds they contain. To compensate for such variation, the herb is standardized. This concentrates the major active ingredients, and the herb extract can be consistent from batch to batch.

Q: *If I decide to try herbal medicine, should I tell my doctor what I'm taking? Will herbs and pharmaceuticals conflict with each other?*

Duke: You should tell your doctor, and your doctor will probably tell you to quit taking herbs. Then find another doctor. Herbs are real medicine, and they will interact with other medicines. I don't tell my doctor, because I know what I'm doing. However, I don't advise other people to do the same. Find a doctor who knows about herbs.

Q: *There has been a lot of news stories about "dangerous herbs," and this scares some people away. Are there dangerous herbs on the shelves?*

Duke: They're generally not for sale in good herb stores. They've been flagged by responsible people. But somebody, somewhere is going to be allergic to anything. So if you're taking a new drug or a new herb or a new food, watch yourself. For example, I would take the herb chaparral myself, yet I wouldn't recommend it to anyone, so I won't get sued. Most medicines will upset the liver enzymes in most people; well, so does chaparral. We've blown the bugle so loud on some of these herbs, and they're really not so bad. Chamomile has been most misunderstood. There are so few cases of chamomile allergic reactions, yet the warnings about chamomile causing allergic reactions have made big news.

However, I caution against ephedra, except under the advice of a physician. Licorice and ephedra can both raise the blood pressure. *Cascara sagrada,* like most laxatives, can be habit-forming.

Q: *If I only have time to learn about ten herbs, which ones should they be?*

Duke: My favorites are celery seed (I take it for gout), St. John's wort, feverfew, ginkgo, echinacea, garlic, ginger, saw palmetto, evening primrose, billberry, kava, and turmeric. That's more than ten, but those are the important ones. I think we'll be hearing a lot in the news in the near future about the benefits of kava and turmeric. Those will probably be the two next most popular herbs. Turmeric is an anti-inflammatory useful for just about everything. Kava's getting a lot of attention for its relaxant properties. However, the one herb that's going to spare Americans the most misery is echinacea.

Q: *What is your personal favorite herb?*

Duke: I take celery seed for gout, and it has saved me a lot of misery.

Q: *Where is herbal medicine going? Will it go mainstream?*

Duke: We're on the crest of a wave. I predict it won't be long before most people start taking herbs in preference to many of the synthetics pushed on them. The trouble is, many components from herbs are getting isolated and are being sold pure, and that's a problem. The FDA will cause problems with that. A new law says you can sell any constituent of any plant, like plant estrogen. This will become a problem. It's just like pycnogenol. Our ancestors never took that in purified form without its other components. It may throw something else out of whack.

We don't want the silver bullet approach, whether it comes from plants or synthetics. It will throw off the ratios in our body that we don't even know about yet. But after we get through that problem, herbal medicine is here to stay. It's just going to get more and more popular. A lot of people are being helped by herbs, or they wouldn't be coming back for more.

WHICH FORM DO YOU TAKE?

You'll find herbs in numerous forms on the shelves of your natural products store. These include dry bulk herbs, herbal tea preparations, crude or pulverized herbs in tablets or capsules (but not extracted), tinctures (herbs steeped in alcohol or another solvent), liquid extracts that are usually alcohol based or glycerine based, and solid extracts in capsule or tablet form (the liquid is completely removed). You'll also find standardized and non-standardized herbs.

Generally, all forms have both benefits and disadvantages. There are several informative books to help you make your decision about which herb form is best for you. Teas are a popular and time-tested way to take medicinal herbs: the herbs are in a solution that helps your body absorb the active ingredient. When you take a capsule or tablet, you don't have to taste the herb (an advantage in some cases), and they're convenient. Liquid extracts and tinctures are the most potent form; thus, small doses are as effective as larger doses of the same herb in another form.

HERBS AND THEIR USES

Billberry *(Vaccinium myrtillus):* visual and vascular disorders

Celery seed *(Apium graveolens):* arthritis, gout

Chamomile *(Matricaria chamomilla):* insomnia, nervousness

Echinacea *(Echinacea* spp.*):* colds, depressed immunity, flu

Evening primrose *(Oenothera biennis):* arthritis, benign prostatic hyperplasia (BPH), eczema, PMS

Feverfew *(Tanacetum parthenium):* headache, migraine

Garlic *(Allium sativum):* high blood pressure, infections

Ginseng *(Panax ginseng):* low energy, low or high blood pressure, poor appetite

Ginkgo *(Ginkgo biloba):* geriatric dementia, impotence

Ginger *(Zingiberis officinalis):* colds, morning sickness, motion sickness, nausea

Kava kava *(Piper methysticum):* insomnia, nervousness

Saw palmetto *(Serenoa repens):* BPH

St. John's wort *(Hypericum perforatum):* arthritis, depression, insomnia

Stinging nettle *(Urtica dioica):* arthritis, BPH, hay fever

Sources: *The Green Pharmacy* by James Duke, Ph.D., and *Natural Healing with Herbs* by Humbart Santillo, N.D., et al.

Standardized herb extracts are popular and still surrounded by controversy. Traditional herbalists believe standardization yields products that are far from the natural whole herbs on which the herbalists' tradition is based. Proponents of standardized extracts point out that herbs, even from the same farm, vary in potency from season to season. Standardization assures that every time you take an herb, its effects will be predictable because it contains an exact, standardized amount of active herb ingredients. This is especially beneficial in a research setting, where the amount of active herb component that each subject receives must be carefully controlled.

With some herbs, however, it's impossible to track down the active ingredient. For example, ginger has been tested and evaluated in different forms for its antinausea effects. Although several components have been found to be active, none of them compares to the activity found in the ginger root itself, which contains a combination of all compounds.

ENDANGERED HERBS

United Plant Savers (UPS), a nonprofit group dedicated to saving medicinal herbs in danger of being overharvested, has compiled the UPS At-Risk List. Plants on this list are presently in decline due to expanding popularity and shrinking habitat and range. The herbs listed include American ginseng *(Panax quinquefolius),* black cohosh *(Cimicifuga racemosa),* echinacea *(Echinacea* spp.), goldenseal *(Hydrastis canadensis),* kava kava *(Piper methysticum),* and wild yam *(Dioscorea villosa).*

UPS is not calling for a moratorium on the use of these herbs; rather, they're initiating programs, both practical and educational, designed to preserve these important wild medicinal plants. For a complete list and more information, call (802) 479-9825.

Chapter 11

Homeopathy
Safe and Simple Medicine

omeopathy, a system of medicine and healing developed nearly two
centuries ago by a German physician, is based on the principle of
"like cures like." (Everyone who has ever had a tetanus shot or other
form of vaccination is familiar with this concept.) To immunize patients
against a disease, vaccinations contain small doses of agents that actually cause
the disease. Homeopathic remedies, on the other hand, stimulate the body's
natural immune and healing responses. The remedies are derived from dilu-
tions of plants, minerals, and animals and taken in minute doses.

The concept of more "like cures like" means that the same substances
causing a particular set of symptoms in a healthy person can cure the same
or similar symptoms in a person who is ill. This law of similars dates back
more than 5,000 years to the ancient medical texts of China and India. Hippocrates, in 400 B.C., also referred to this same idea. Today, modern research
is validating the positive effects of homeopathic treatment.

"Homeopathy has been used therapeutically in this country for 150
years. It has an impeccable reputation for safety," explains Dana Ullman,
M.P.H., founder of Homeopathic Educational Services and author of *Homeopathic Medicine for Children and Infants* and *Everybody's Guide to Homeopathic
Medicines*. Research has proven homeopathy's effectiveness, including a
1994 study published in the British medical journal *The Lancet* that
reported 81 percent of asthma patients given homeopathic medicines
showed improvement.

Approved by the FDA, many of these natural medicines have been used in the United States since the turn of the century. Today, homeopathy is an accepted form of medicine in many parts of the world, including Great Britain, France, Germany, Greece, India, and South America.

Homeopathic remedies are invaluable to a parent with children vulnerable to illnesses from flu to colds to chickenpox. Though it's best to work with a homeopathic physician who can help you find the right remedy for an illness, when you're on your own, you can do pretty well by referring to the materia medica at the back of this book (see Appendix A).

Because these remedies are side effect–free, they tend to be my first choice when treating my daughter. If she has a burning fever, I'll try *Ferrum phosphorous. Nux vomica* has often settled her upset stomach. Chamomilla helps her go to sleep and is a great remedy for teething. By learning just these few remedies and keeping them in your medicine cabinet, you can avoid some trips to the doctor's office as well as some sleepless nights.

HOMEOPATHY FOR HYPERACTIVE CHILDREN

One of the most impressive uses of homeopathy is with children who have been diagnosed with attention deficit hyperactivity disorder (ADHD) or attention deficit disorder (ADD). Here is one child's story:

When Sherrie entered kindergarten, the teachers immediately labeled her a "problem child" because of her ceaseless fidgeting and inability to stop talking. By the time she was in sixth grade, Sherrie's bewildered parents put her on Ritalin, a prescription stimulant used to treat ADHD and ADD. The drug gave Sherrie hives and made her feel as though she didn't know herself. But without Ritalin, she was unable to focus on anything from simple conversations to homework.

After five years on Ritalin, Sherrie's family physician referred her to homeopathic physicians Judyth Reichenberg Ullman, N.D., and Robert Ullman, N.D., who run the Northwest Center for Homeopathic Medicine in Edmonds, Washington. The Ullmans met Sherrie, interviewed her, and gave her a single dose of a homeopathic remedy called *Veratrum album*. Five weeks later, Sherrie was showing major improvements in her ability to concentrate. She was able to sit still without fidgeting and to control her impulsive talking. Sherrie told her prescribing physician she no longer wanted to take Ritalin.

After discontinuing Ritalin, and after taking only one dose of *Veratrum album,* her grades improved, and Sherrie's parents reported that her behavior drastically improved. Over the next year and a half, Sherrie needed only two more doses of *Veratrum album,* then discontinued it completely because she was doing so well.

THE ADHD AND ADD EPIDEMIC

ADHD, once called hyperkinesis or minimal brain dysfunction, and ADD are the most common mental disorders among children, according to information posted on the Web site of the National Institute of Mental Health (NIMH), the federal agency that supports nationwide research on the brain, mental illness, and mental health. These disorders affect 3 to 5 percent of all children, and perhaps as many as two million American children. NIMH reports that two to three times more boys than girls are affected.

ADHD is a diagnosis applied to children and adults who consistently display three common behaviors over a significant period of time (at least six months): inattention, hyperactivity, and impulsivity. ADD is a diagnosis applied to children or adults who display inattention and impulsivity without hyperactivity. *Inattention* is defined as having a hard time keeping focused on any one thing and becoming bored with a task after only a few minutes. *Hyperactivity* is defined as intense restlessness, fidgeting, and inability to stay still. An impulsive person is one who is unable to curb immediate reactions to things, makes inappropriate comments, and is unable to wait for things. These behaviors must be displayed excessively, pervasively, and over a long period of time in order for the child or adult to be diagnosed with ADHD or ADD.

According to NIMH, the causes of ADHD and ADD are unknown. For a while, scientists believed that all attention disorders and learning disabilities were caused by minor head injuries or undetectable damage to the brain brought on by early infection or complications at birth. Based on this theory, both disorders were first called minimal brain damage or minimal brain dysfunction. Scientists later rejected this theory because it could explain only a small number of cases.

In 1982, the National Institutes of Health (NIH) held a major scientific conference to discuss causes of ADHD and ADD. After studying the data, scientists concluded that diet (such as artificial flavorings, preservatives, and sugars) was not responsible for most cases of ADHD or ADD. Many alternative practitioners disagree with this finding, however. Ullman notes that in her practice she has found some correlation between the disorders and sugar and food additive consumption. "Dietary approaches undoubtedly do work for some children, but not for many others," she explains.

Meanwhile, scientists at NIMH have used a positive emission tomography scanner to observe the brain and found important differences between people who have ADHD (or ADD) and those who don't. In people with ADHD or ADD, the brain areas that control attention are less active than in people without ADHD or ADD. Researchers are still unable to determine why this occurs. Scientists also are investigating the theory that a mother's use of cigarettes, alcohol, or other drugs during pregnancy may have damaging effects on the brain of the unborn child. Many children born with a condition called fetal alcohol syndrome, caused by a mother's excessive use of alcohol during pregnancy, also exhibit hyperactivity, inattention, and impulsivity.

The three most common medications prescribed for children with ADHD and ADD are methylphenidate (Ritalin), dextroamphetamine (Dexedrine), and pemoline (Cylert). These medications belong to the class of drugs known as stimulants and can be addictive. These stimulants don't cure the disorder; they only temporarily control the symptoms. For example, the calming benefits of Ritalin last only four hours. NIMH lists side effects to Ritalin that include weight loss, diminished appetite, slowed growth rate, and sleep disorders.

A KINDER, GENTLER TREATMENT

"We've treated over 1,400 children [with ADD and ADHD] homeopathically and seen many cases where there's been a dramatic turnaround," says Judyth Ullman. "Homeopathy treats the whole person, and it zeroes in on what's most unique about each person. Children with ADD and ADHD are very unique, so it's an excellent match."

Homeopathy treats ADD and ADHD effectively by bringing the individual into balance, she explains. "Homeopaths treat people with ADD [or ADHD], not the ADD itself. The treatment is considered safe, without the side effects of Ritalin and other medications; and the effects lasts for months or years rather than four hours. It's also very inexpensive."

One of the common questions that Ullman is asked by the parents of ADD and ADHD children is if Ritalin and homeopathy can be administered together. This is a decision between the patient and the prescribing physician, she says. However, homeopathy can be given simultaneously with Ritalin, and as symptoms disappear, the Ritalin can be phased out. If parents are afraid to give up Ritalin, we can treat the child while they're still on Ritalin. As soon as we see that the homeopathy has really worked, we work with the prescribing physician to take the child off Ritalin."

Homeopathy doesn't just treat symptoms, says Ullman. "We look at the whole person. ADD and ADHD are not acute conditions, such as colds, that can be treated symptomatically. They're chronic conditions which must be treated by trained, professional homeopaths." Homeopathy works on a deep and lasting level. "It's not a quick and temporary fix, like Ritalin," she states.

Ullman's career as an ADHD specialist began unintentionally ten years ago. One of her family-practice patients was a foster mother who adopted very difficult children and began bringing them to Ullman's clinic to be treated homeopathically. "Some of these children had been abused, and some had ADHD. I had some really wonderful results with those children. So I began presenting their cases at conferences, and it generated a lot of interest from other physicians. Now it's my specialty. My husband and I actually do family practice, but we get mostly ADD and ADHD kids because of our successes with them."

Ullman has plenty of compassion for parents who are being pressured by school officials to put their children on Ritalin. "You have to do what's in your heart. I think it's important not to be pressured to make decisions. We offer an alternative to Ritalin. But we don't criticize people who put their children on Ritalin. They're doing what they think is best for their kids. However, if you're going to use homeopathy for your ADD or ADHD child, you must consult with a homeopathic practitioner."

Chapter 12

Flower Essences
Helping Children Stay Healthy

When I first heard about flower remedies in the 1980s, I was skeptical. The concept seemed vague to me. I couldn't understand how a diluted flower essence could bring about deep and lasting emotional change. I began trying them on myself, with good results. Still, I thought it might be chalked up to the power of suggestion.

When my daughter was four years old, I went through a painful divorce from her father. I took her to counseling and spent many hours talking to her about the pain we were both feeling. Out of desperation, I started taking the flower essence walnut, which is used to help people through a painful transition. I gave it to Sarah as well. This is when my deep respect for these remedies began. She had an almost instant beneficial effect after taking the remedy, and I felt better as well. Today these remedies are a part of our lives, and we take them to help us get through difficult situations. I'd like to share the following story with you.

When Nancy Buono's second child was born, her first child, then four years old, got sick and stayed sick for a year. This formerly healthy little girl (who appeared to get along fabulously with her new brother) suddenly had raging ear infections, high fevers, and eventually shingles. "I tried everything to help her—from herbs and nutrition to conventional medicine. Nothing worked. When she got shingles at five years old, I knew we were in trouble," remembers Buono.

A friend brought Buono some Bach flower essences—diluted plant extracts that address emotional imbalances, believed to be at the root of all disease. "I took one look at holly [given for jealousy] and realized that my daughter was jealous. We had been so close until her baby brother was born. She was too sweet to act outright jealous, so it made her sick instead."

Buono gave four drops of holly, four times a day, to her daughter. Within one week the shingles were gone, and her overall health improved rapidly. Buono believes the flower essences helped her daughter resolve the sibling jealousy that was the underlying cause of her ill health.

Simply put, flower essences are dilute essences of flowers designed to treat emotional distress. They're used not to treat physical illness directly, but to treat the individual's negative emotions, such as fear and worry. However, they often have a positive effect on overall health as well. "It's important to understand that holly is not a remedy for shingles. The flower essences resolve emotional issues and turn negative emotions such as jealousy into positive ones such as love," explains Buono, now a flower essence practitioner for sixteen years in Tempe, Arizona. "And when the emotions are in balance, the body has more energy freed up to heal itself."

Dr. Edward Bach, a British immunologist and homeopath, and creator of the Bach flower essences, believed that disease is a manifestation of the conflict between the personality and the soul. Buono elaborates, "Our outer self gets pushed and pulled by desires, and our inner self knows who we truly are. The flowers reconnect the inner and outer parts of ourselves and, thus, eliminate the dis-ease."

By changing our negative emotions into positive ones, for example, from fear to love, we rediscover our natural balance and thus can prevent disease, explains Barbara Mazzarella, author of *Bach Flower Remedies for Children*. "If we use flowers to correct negative states and reestablish equilibrium in children, we may well end up with fewer distressed adults," she explains.

"Flowers help us peel back the layers so we can get to our true selves, which are loving, caring, considerate, and strong," says flower essence practitioner and educator Patricia Meyer, who has worked with flower essences for twenty-eight years in San Mateo, California. "We're working from the heart when we work with the flower essences."

FLOWER DOCTOR

In the 1930s, Dr. Bach became dissatisfied with medicine and its emphasis on injections and foreign substances introduced into the body. He believed that physical illness was a manifestation of an emotional imbalance, and that all human beings contained the potential to heal themselves if they worked within the perfect pattern of nature.

As a lover of nature, he recognized that certain flowers contained positive energies that could help transform our human negative emotions, such as fear, into love. Eventually, he abandoned his thriving medical practice and moved to his grandparents' cottage in Wales, where he created the thirty-eight flower essences we know today as the Bach Flower Remedies.

He began his work by meticulously observing the plants and their traits. He kept journals describing each plant's characteristic, such as late-blooming or showy, hardy or fragile, and sensitive. He developed an elaborate method of cultivation whereby the flower is cut in a way that prevents the collector's hand from touching the flower. The clipped flower is caught in a crystal bowl of spring water held just below the plant. The remedy is created from the blossom of the flower, which is believed to be the most connected to the essence of the plant. He believed the flower essences could bring out our loving natures—and thus bring us gently back to health and harmony.

Bach's thirty-eight essences address seven areas of emotional discord: fear, uncertainty, loneliness, insufficient interest in present circumstances, oversensitivity to outer influences, despondency, and excessive concern for the welfare of others. The North American Flower Essence Society, working from Bach's knowledge, has since added another thirty-four remedies, bringing the total to seventy-two.

Flower essence practitioners consider the remedies vibrational in nature, much like homeopathic remedies. They are highly dilute substances, like homeopathic remedies, and their effect does not come from any direct biochemical interaction within the physiology of the body. Rather, they work with energy fields—something quite foreign to Western scientists. In fact, flower remedies are considered to be catalysts that stimulate the inner transformation process. And the good news is, they're side effect–free.

The idea of working with energy fields is more than 5,000 years old. Traditional Chinese medicine is based on a system of energetic forces called *chi* (vital life force). Western medicine has been slow to grasp the idea of energy fields, and because there have been no clinical studies into the effectiveness of flower remedies, Western medicine considers them harmless and worthless.

The proof of their potency is in the results, says Buono. Those results can be seen very clearly in children, she adds. "The essences are particularly effective with children. Kids don't have so many emotional blocks or years of emotional experience to work through. You can see dramatic results quickly."

Meyer, whose practice includes numerous children, agrees. "Children have fewer layers to peel back to get to their true selves. It's easier to work through the emotional trauma with a child than with an adult."

The flower essences work beautifully with children of all ages. "With infants, you can put drops on their pulse points, their forehead, or behind their ears," Buono says. "And with teenagers, flowers can have remarkable results. Crabapple is great for a teenager overly concerned about her appearance. Or if they're being critical and intolerant, try beech. And if they procrastinate and don't do their homework until midnight, give them hornbeam. It can really make a difference."

Buono has been treating numerous ADD children. "I just treated an eight-year-old boy whose doctor wanted to put him on Ritalin. We identified that he was irritable, easily frustrated, and tended to daydream. I made a mixture of impatiens, heather, and clematis for him. He showed good improvement within a few days. His teachers were happy. Now, of course, we're uncovering some of the deeper issues, like lack of self-confidence and working with that. You have to keep peeling off the layers. It's part of the healing process."

Meyer believes that birth trauma can cause learning and attention span problems. "The flowers can heal the birth trauma so the child can focus in the present moment. Flowers get to the source of the problem and heal the underlying pain, rather than just dealing with the effects of the pain, the way Ritalin does."

When treating children, Buono suggests making a treatment bottle from a 1-ounce amber bottle nearly filled with spring water. "Add two drops of

FLOWERS FOR CHILDREN

Beech: for children intolerant of parents or others.

Cherry plum: for temper tantrums.

Clematis: for the daydreamer; helps bring the child to the present moment.

Crabapple: for the child obsessed with appearances.

Goldenrod: for children easily influenced by peers to engage in inappropriate behavior.

Impatiens: for impatient children.

Heather: for children easily irritated by others.

Holly: for sibling rivalry, jealousy.

Hornbeam: to reduce procrastination regarding chores or school-work.

Rescue remedy: a combination of essences good for shock, trauma, and teething pain.

Star of Bethlehem: for coping with loss, such as death of a pet or loved one.

Walnut: helps the child move through a difficult transition such as divorce.

Source: Nancy Buono and Patricia Meyer.

each prescribed flower essence to the treatment bottle. Give the child four drops, four times a day," she explains.

Buono uses as many as four different essences per treatment, and she doesn't use a preservative such as brandy. "It doesn't taste good, and if you keep the dropper from touching the tongue, the remedy will last about three weeks."

Remember, you can't overdose with flower essences. "If you want faster, more dramatic results, give more drops. If you want a gentle shift, give less. There are no harmful side effects to worry about," says Buono. "It's complementary medicine in its truest sense. It works with any other modality, from herbs to antibiotics. And it works on our deepest levels, where true healing can take place."

People are just beginning to realize that only through flower essences can our spiritual selves be healed, Meyer asserts. "The medical doctor can heal us physically, the psychiatrist or therapist can heal us mentally or emotionally, but only the flower essences can heal us spiritually."

Meyer believes that flowers dramatically improve our health because they heal our spiritual pain, which is the basis of disease. "If you have cancer and you don't want to be in this world anymore, you can't heal. Flowers can awaken your vitality, your interest in life. Then your body can heal itself."

The effects of flower essences can be subtle but powerful. Meyer explains, "Sometimes people take them for a while and don't know if they're doing any good. Then suddenly they'll find themselves responding positively in a situation that used to elicit a negative response from them. They're not hooked by the same hooks as before. Flowers are truly gifts from God for our healing. They teach us to love life."

Chapter 13

Chinese Medicine

Before my daughter was born, I spent years getting acupuncture and Chinese medicine treatments from David Scrimgeour, R.Ac. We worked on issues such as stress, migraine headaches, skin rashes, and the usual array of colds and flu. I found Chinese medicine to be a profound healing tool. After Sarah was born, I learned about all the ways David could help her with acupressure, herbs, and other Chinese medicine techniques.

One of my favorite stories is about the time David stopped an extremely bad cough. For two nights, my daughter's coughing was so severe it triggered episodes of vomiting. Her pediatrician said it could be a mild case of pertussis (whooping cough) and that we should watch her carefully. (There is no conventional cure for pertussis.) I took her to see David. He pressed on certain points of her body with mild acupressure, took her pulse, looked at her tongue, and then mixed up an herbal liquid tincture containing Chinese herbs. I was instructed to give her a dropperful every three hours. I started her on the herbs immediately.

She never coughed again, slept through the night without any trouble, and was virtually well the next day. I took her back to her pediatrician, who was very impressed and wanted to know the name of my practitioner.

EXPERT ADVICE

Here, David Scrimgeour shares his insights into using Chinese medicine to treat children.

"Oriental medicine has existed as a complete system of health care for well over 2,000 years. Over this time period, it has developed many safe and effective treatments for a vast array of children's disorders. One of the most important and unique features of this system that makes it so effective is found in the concept of strengthening, or tonifying, the body. This concept does not really exist in conventional Western medicine but is essential to understanding Oriental medicine. In essence, it is a system of balance: where there is weakness or deficiency, it is imperative to strengthen, and where there is excess, it is imperative to sedate or remove the excess. For example, in this system, a bacterial infection will tend to look like an excess with redness, fever, swelling, pain, etc. The treatment will focus on removing the excess by taking the heat out of the system with specific herbal formulas and/or subtle bodywork techniques based on the system of acupuncture. The focus, then, is on assisting the body through the immune system and other environmental or lifestyle influences—for example, diet—to bring about balance. It does not focus merely on removing a pathogen, as do antibiotics and most conventional Western treatments.

"Oriental medicine offers a viable alternative to conventional care for children in a number of areas, particularly when dealing with chronic illness. Some of its important features are as follows:

1. *Oriental medicine tends to have few, if any, side effects.* This is due to the wisdom of using well-balanced herbal formulas that work *with* the body and not against it. Within each formula are often found herbs that help soften the harsh effects of another herb or enhance the effects of certain other herbs. In other words, the combinations are synergistic.

2. *Oriental medicine tends to be more effective than many conventional strategies in treating chronic illness.* We are not talking about life-threatening disease here but many of the common, long-term, and hard-to-treat illnesses such as asthma, chronic ear infections, headaches, digestive disturbances, etc. As mentioned above, this is due to the emphasis on strengthening the body as well as the ability to work well with the whole system, since most chronic illnesses, according to Oriental medicine, are in fact systemic problems.

3. *The approach is thorough.* If a child is treated properly with Oriental medicine, there are usually no recurrences, as often happens after using antibiotics. Because of its emphasis on treating the whole body, strengthening the immune system is typically a part of any treatment

plan, which leads to longer-lasting and better effects of treatment. For example, in Japanese medicine, it is known that it is very important to completely eradicate a cold or virus from the body. This implies the tonification, or strengthening, of the body to prevent the return of the illness and to boost the body's ability to rid it completely of the pathogen.

4. *Oriental medicine addresses prevention.* It should be obvious how important this can be. In other words, it is not enough in the practice of Oriental medicine to simply eradicate symptoms. It is essential to understand the root cause of a problem and to work with the body to change it or get it out of the system.

5. *Oriental medicine is tried and true.* As stated above, Oriental medicine has been around for a very long time, and the treatments used are well established as being safe and effective with hundreds of years of experience to prove it."

A common question with regard to the treatment of children using Oriental medicine is, "What does it involve and how is it done?" Basically there are two aspects to the delivery system. The first, and probably the most widely practiced, is the prescribing of herbal formulas as mentioned above. These are typically given either in liquid as tinctures or extracts, or in powders or granules that are freeze-dried from traditional cooked formulas. Some children prefer the liquids mixed with water or juice, and others prefer the powders, which are typically mixed with food such as applesauce or cereal. A wide variety of formulas are available in both forms. The second, a less commonly practiced form of Oriental medicine for children is *Tui Na* (a Chinese form of massage therapy) or *Shonishin* (a Japanese form of acupuncture therapy that employs small tools used in a massage-type fashion that works according to the same principles as acupuncture, using special points and meridians). Most children like this gentle approach and can benefit greatly from these hands-on techniques that tend to be calming and soothing.

Also commonly asked is what types of conditions are seen in the Oriental medicine clinic. The conditions tend to be very much like those seen in a general pediatric clinic. The common problems in the list below are all treated with effectiveness by properly trained practitioners. (A note of caution: if there is any concern as to a particular diagnosis or severity of a condition, it is always recommended that the child be seen first by a pediatrician.)

- Ear infections (especially the chronic ones)
- Sinus infections
- Colds
- Cough
- Bladder infections
- Allergies
- Headaches
- Stomachaches
- Insomnia
- Asthma

In summary, Oriental medicine can, in many cases, be a viable alternative to conventional care and can be received without side effects and can often produce better, longer-lasting results. It is especially worth considering for those cases that have not responded well to conventional care and where a resolution to a more systemic type of problem is needed.

A further note regarding use of herbal formulas: In most cases, over-the-counter herbal formulas are safe and often effective, but caution should be used in purchasing formulas from China, as there has been some difficulty with ensuring the contents of some products. In general, it is advisable to seek the help of a qualified practitioner of Oriental medicine who can make a proper assessment of the condition and then recommend the appropriate formula with the appropriate dose for the individual child. Another common problem with over-the-counter formulas is that their labels tend to recommend lower than clinically used doses, which often results in undermedicating with little or no effect.

FINDING A PRACTITIONER

A number of qualities should be sought out in finding the right practitioner for you and your child. As in any field, the most important is experience. Some of it has to do with training, and some of it has to do with the type and number of children the practitioner has seen. In addition, if the practitioner has children of her own, she obviously will have a better understanding of children and their behavior and needs.

It is also important to know what kind of training a person has had. This can be stated in years of schooling, number of hours taken, years in practice, and additional educational training. The standard in California is basically the highest in the United States at the present time and has been fairly uniform for the last ten years, with most schools following the same or a similar curriculum. There is a fair amount of emphasis on Western medicine, which can be of benefit to understanding an already given diagnosis. Therefore, you can be assured that someone who has been educated in California in recent years will most likely possess the basic skills needed to be a competent practitioner. Besides the California standard, practitioners who have passed the exam in herbal medicine given by the National Commission for the Certification of Acupuncture and Oriental Medicine (NCCAOM) are designated Certified Herbologists. This is typically written as C.H. or Dipl. C.H.

The final quality in finding a practitioner is rapport. You and your child need to feel comfortable and confident in a practitioner no matter what his training. If you follow these basic criteria, you should be able to get the help you need.

Chapter 14

Nutritional Supplementation for Kids

I t's not easy making sure your child is getting all the nutrients she needs. The younger a child is, the more control we as parents have over what she eats. But as children grow older and begin attending school and spending more time away from home, we can't be sure they're getting all the important vitamins and minerals they require for a healthy, growing body that will support them into adulthood. That's why most parents turn to a quality multiple vitamin and mineral supplement that covers a child's recommended daily allowances (RDAs) as nutritional insurance to prevent deficiencies. Vitamins and minerals are mandatory not only for proper growth and development but also to keep children healthy and robust so they can fight off an illness before it can take hold. Many experts such as Jeffrey Bland, Ph.D., believe that much larger dosages than the RDAs are required for disease prevention and healthy maintenance.

Vitamin and mineral supplements come from either natural food sources or are manufactured synthetically. Synthetic and natural vitamins and minerals have identical chemical structures and are thought to act similarly in the body. There is controversy as to which is more effectively absorbed and used. Natural proponents such as Michael Murray, N.D., believe that natural food source vitamins are utilized more efficiently by the body.

Supplements destined for the mainstream market use refined sugars, artificial sweeteners, and artificial colors to appeal to children. If you decide that a multiple vitamin-mineral is right for your child, be sure to purchase a brand that uses only natural fruit juices and sweeteners, such as honey or rice syrup. Make sure it doesn't have preservatives or artificial colors. Liquid vitamins are appropriate during the first year, followed by chewable vitamins. As they grow, many children are able to swallow pills and capsules. Powdered nutritional formulas can be added to foods as another option. I firmly believe that your natural foods store is the place to shop for supplements. After my more than ten years of working as a natural health editor, I can tell you that you'll find a higher quality product in natural food stores such as Whole Foods or through Web sites such as healthshop.com than you will in a mainstream grocery store or drugstore.

VITAMINS AND MINERALS

Vitamins are essential micronutrients required by a child's body for normal metabolism, growth, and development. They are either fat soluble (A, D, E, and K) or water soluble (B vitamins and C). The B vitamins include B1 (thiamine), B2 (riboflavin), B6 (pyridoxine), pantothenic acid, niacin, biotin, folic acid (folate), and B12 (cobalamin). The RDA—the amount an average child needs each day to stay healthy—has been determined for each vitamin. Consuming too little or too much of certain vitamins can lead to nutritional disorders.

Important as they are, vitamins cannot help without their low-profile, less flamboyant counterparts—minerals. For example:

- Vitamins cannot be assimilated without the aid of minerals.
- The body can manufacture a few vitamins, but it cannot manufacture a single mineral.
- All tissues and internal fluids contain varying quantities of minerals.
- Minerals act as catalysts for many biological reactions within the body, such as muscle response, transmission of messages through the nervous system, production of hormones, digestion, and utilization of nutrients in foods.

Some minerals—sodium, chloride, potassium, calcium, phosphorus, and magnesium—are considered macronutrients because they are needed by the body in relatively large quantities. Other minerals are called micronutrients, or trace minerals, because they are needed by the body in small quantities.

These include iron, zinc, copper, manganese, molybdenum, selenium, iodine, and fluoride.

INFANT REQUIREMENTS

Optimal nutrition for infants, both before and after birth, is an area of research that is still unfolding. A study reported in the *British Medical Journal* demonstrated for the first time that early nutrition can significantly influence mental ability later in life. Researchers found that premature infants who were fed a standard milk formula rather than a nutrient-enriched formula had reduced verbal IQ scores by the time they were seven to eight years old. The results were particularly evident in boys. The authors noted that early nutrition during a child's development can have lifetime effects on health and performance.

After the post–World War II, formula-feeding revolution, mothers are happily returning to breast-feeding, the healthiest choice for a child. Breast milk is a substance uniquely formulated to meet an infant's growth requirements. Initially, breast milk is high in fat and fatty acids, which are important to the early development needs of the brain and the immune and nervous systems. Later, the fat content of breast milk decreases and is replaced with protein and carbohydrates, which support the rapid growth and development experienced during this age.

Breast milk also has more iron, vitamins A and C, niacin, potassium, and the right amino acids for growth than any natural or formulated substitute. In fact, its precise mix of enzymes, long-chain fatty acids, and proteins is so complex it cannot be duplicated exactly using the modified milk of other mammals or created from mixtures of plant-based materials. The essential fatty acids in breast milk are fundamental for an infant's neural development. Evidence suggests that term and premature infants require the omega-3 essential fatty acid DHA (docosahexaenoic acid) for ideal growth and development. "Essential fatty acids are utilized by all body tissues, but especially by the brain," explains Michael Murray, N.D. "They are necessary to the manufacture of structural components of cell membranes and important hormonelike substances known as prostaglandins."

Essential fatty acids are more like vitamins than fats. They are sometimes referred to as vitamin F because they are so important in the diet. They are essential because the body cannot manufacture them; they must come from the diet. Essential fatty acids fall into two categories: omega-3 and omega-6. In addition to supporting proper growth and development, essential fatty acids perform a variety of functions in the body:

- They transport the fat-soluble vitamins (A, D, E, and K).
- They help manage cholesterol.
- They regulate body temperature.
- They help control blood pressure.
- They are essential for healthy skin, hair, and nails.

After a baby is born, the primary source of DHA is breast milk. Although researchers have yet to define how DHA affects brain functions including memory and learning, they know DHA is required for the development of the cerebral cortex—the thin, folded layers of the brain's hemispheres that house billions of brain cells.

Numerous studies show that babies who are breast-fed have better brain development than their formula-fed counterparts. A recent study in *The Lancet* corroborated these findings. Researchers found significantly higher amounts of DHA in the brains of breast-fed babies than in those of formula-fed babies. Higher concentrations of DHA in the brains of breast-fed infants may explain their improved neurodevelopment when compared with formula-fed infants.

In addition to its important role in brain development, DHA plays a vital function in developing sharpness of vision. DHA is found in high concentrations in the photoreceptors of the retina and supplies lipids (fats) to the retinal membrane. It has been noted that when levels of DHA are too low, abnormal visual functioning occurs.

Many infant formulas contain little or no DHA. According to a report in *Archives of Disease in Childhood,* even the breast milk of vegan women, who eat no animal products, contains substantially greater amounts of DHA than cow-milk formulas. If breast-feeding isn't possible, a study in the same journal recommends that a minimum daily requirement of 30 milligrams of DHA be added to the formulas of term infants to prevent a brain deficiency of the essential fatty acid. Murray recommends adding 200 milligrams of DHA a day to infant formula.

Some physicians believe a healthy baby on breast milk does not need additional supplements. However, most parents are more comfortable giving a simple supplement that covers an infant's RDAs. A liquid vitamin-mineral supplement is appropriate for the first year. Parents also should be aware that infants can overdose on some vitamins, according to Elson Haas, M.D. Vitamin A toxicity is probably most common. Haas recommends that parents not overuse vitamins A and D, cod liver oil (which is high in both A and D), or the minerals calcium, phosphorus, and iron.

NUTRITIONAL INSURANCE

Children are constantly growing, and their nutritional needs change often. Between ages two and twelve, it's important to instill good eating habits. A healthful diet featuring fresh fruits and vegetables, whole grains, lean meats, and low-fat dairy products can help children make good food choices as they grow older and eat away from home. Because it is virtually impossible for children (and even adults) to get all the nutrients they need for optimal health from diet alone, supplemental vitamins and minerals are a good idea. "While we want to stress the importance of eating a healthy diet, the fact of the matter is that children do not always eat healthfully," said Murray. "Nutritional supplements can be used to fortify the nutrient intake."

Childhood eating habits have changed over the past few decades, and not for the better, as the following research shows.

- The U.S. Department of Agriculture (USDA) recently released a Food Guide Pyramid for Young Children aimed at ages two to six. It contains basically the same information as the main Food Guide Pyramid but is more kid-friendly. The USDA is promoting this pyramid because research has found that most children do not meet nutritional guidelines, especially for consuming enough fruit, vegetables, grains, and dairy products.

- A study of 168 American preschool children, reported in the *Journal of the American College of Nutrition,* found that none ate the five recommended daily servings of fruits and vegetables. Most children in the study ate less than a half serving of vegetables and only two servings of fruit a day. Plus, about half of the fruit servings were in the form of juice, which contains no fiber and very few nutrients.

- Teachers in several Maryland schools asked teens to keep a food diary for one day. The teachers found that pizza, soda, spaghetti, hamburgers, and french fries were the foods consumed most often by the teens that day.

Jeffrey Bland, Ph.D., founder of Healthcom, Inc., in Gig Harbor, Washington, notes that ample evidence suggests many children suffer from vitamin and mineral deficiencies resulting from their penchant to eat and drink sweet, fried, or salty foods instead of unprocessed natural foods. "Parents can offer their children nutritional insurance in the form of a daily multivitamin/mineral tablet," notes Bland. "This would help ensure proper intake of the critically important nutrients that support growth, development, immune function, and far-ranging functions related to brain chemistry and its control of mood, mind, and behavior."

When children do not meet their nutritional needs, serious problems can result. In the *Journal of the American Medical Association,* a study of adolescents found that teens may be at greater risk for cardiovascular disease later in life due to elevated blood levels of homocysteine, a naturally occurring amino acid that has been linked with a greater risk of heart disease. Researchers found that homocysteine levels, which tend to be higher when folic acid levels are lower, were higher in youngsters who did not take multivitamins. They also discovered elevated levels in boys compared with girls, and higher levels in black children compared with white and Hispanic children. "Our results suggest that multivitamin intake or supplementation with folic acid and possibly vitamin B12 may reduce homocysteine levels, especially for children with extremely high levels," said Dr. Stavroula Osganian, the study's lead researcher.

Several new studies conducted around the globe found that the mineral zinc, which supports the immune system and plays a role in reproductive organ growth and development, also may help prevent infectious diseases. In the United States, babies born prematurely or with low birth weights are at particular risk of zinc deficiency. One of the studies, conducted in India, suggested that giving children zinc reduces their chances of developing respiratory illnesses by 45 percent or more. Another study from Vietnam found that youngsters given zinc were less than half as likely to have respiratory infections than those not given zinc. Among low-birth-weight Brazilian babies, those given 5 milligrams of zinc a day were 33 percent less likely to have a cough than babies not given zinc. A cough is one of the first signs of a respiratory infection.

To be sure your children are getting their share of vitamins and minerals, Murray recommends a good multiple vitamin-mineral formula. He also advises vitamin C in addition to the multiple at the following dosages:

- under age two: 50 milligrams twice daily (can be added to juice or bottle)
- two to six: 100 milligrams twice daily
- six to twelve: 250 milligrams twice daily
- twelve and above: 500 milligrams twice daily

To ensure that children are receiving adequate essential fatty acids, Murray suggests regular consumption of cold-water fish (salmon, mackerel, herring, halibut) and 1 or 2 teaspoons of flaxseed oil daily. Nutritional insurance in the form of a multiple vitamin for toddlers should contain all the B vitamins and the antioxidant vitamins C, E, and A. Haas also recommends basic minerals such as calcium and iron, as well as zinc, magnesium, manganese, and even a little chromium and selenium.

VEGETARIAN CHILDREN

As many parents choose vegetarianism in their search for healthier lifestyles, vegetarian children are becoming more common. If appropriately planned, even vegan diets (those that exclude all products made from animals, including meat, fish, and poultry; milk, cheese and other dairy items; eggs; and honey) can provide adequate nutrition for children, according to the Institute of Food Technologists and the American Dietetic Association. However, since children have higher metabolic rates and consequently higher energy requirements than adults, parents must be aware of a child's different nutritional requirements. Some important nutrients are found predominantly in animal products (iron, vitamin B12, zinc), and these must be included in a child's diet by careful food selection and supplementation. Murray recommends that in addition to a quality multiple vitamin-mineral supplement, vegetarian children should take extra vitamin B12 and zinc. The accompanying table lists RDAs for vegetarian children.

RDAs for Vegetarian Children

Age (years)	Iron (mg)	B12 (mcg)	Zinc (mg)	Calcium (mg)	D (mcg)
0–6 mos.	6	0.3	5	400	7.5
6 mos.–1 yr.	10	0.5	5	600	10
1–3	10	0.7	10	800	10
4–6	10	1.0	10	800	10
7–10	10	1.4	10	800	10

Source: National Resource Council, Recommended Dietary Allowances.

RECOGNIZING SIGNS OF VITAMIN DEFICIENCY

Parents should be aware of the signs of vitamin deficiency in any child. Regular doctor's visits should include questions about the child's diet and food intolerances and an examination of the child for signs of nutritional deficiencies or disorders that interfere with nutrition, such as malabsorption, kidney disease, diarrhea, and metabolic or genetic diseases. A doctor evaluates a child's growth by observing changes in height and weight and comparing them to normal growth curves. Most vitamin deficiencies are rare among infants and children in industrialized countries, but the most common ones are deficiencies of vitamin E, vitamin C, or essential fatty acids. RDAs for children are listed in the following table.

Vitamin E deficiency is relatively common in premature infants. Vitamin E deficiency also may occur in children who have disorders that interfere with fat absorption, such as cystic fibrosis and certain genetic abnormalities. Excessive amounts of iron also may aggravate vitamin E deficiency. The deficiency can be corrected by giving vitamin E supplements.

Infantile scurvy is a condition caused by an inadequate intake of vitamin C, usually resulting from receiving cow's milk formulas, which are deficient in this vitamin and need supplementation. This disease usually occurs between six and twelve months of age. Early symptoms include irritability, poor appetite, and failure to gain weight. Because vitamin C is necessary for the formation of connective tissue (the tissue that holds the body's structures together), scurvy also may cause bone abnormalities in the rib cage and in the long bones of the legs. Scurvy also results in poor wound healing.

RDAs for Children

VITAMINS

Age (years)	Vitamin A (I.U.)	Vitamin D (I.U.)	Vitamin E (I.U.)	Vitamin K (mcg)	Vitamin C (mcg)
0–6 mos.				5	30
6 mos.–1 yr.				10	35
0–1	1,875	200–400	4.5–6.0		
1–3	2,000	200–400	9–10.5	15	40
4–6	1,500	200–400	9–10.5	20	45
7–10	3,500	200–400	9–10.5	30	45

	Thiamine (B1) (mg)	Riboflavin (B2) (mg)	Niacin (B3) (mg)	Pyridoxine (B6) (mg)	Biotin (mg)
0–6 mos.	0.3	0.4	5	0.3	10
6 mos.–1 yr.	0.4	0.5	6	0.6	15
1–3	0.7	0.8	9	1.0	20
4–6	0.9	1.1	12	1.1	25
7–10	1.0	1.2	13	1.4	30

	Pantothenic Acid (B5) (mg)	Folic Acid (mcg)	Cobalamin (B12) (mcg)
0–6 mos.	2	25	0.3
6 mos.–1 yr.	3	35	0.5
1–3	3–4	50	0.7
4–6	3–4	75	1.0
7–10	4–5	100	1.4

Continued

MINERALS

Age (years)	Calcium (mg)	Magnesium (mg)	Potassium (mg)	Zinc (mg)	Chromium (mcg)
0–6 mos.	400	40	500		10–40
6 mos.–1 yr.	600	60	700		20–60
0–1				5	
1–3	800	80	1,000	10	20–80
4–6	800	120	1,400	10	30–120
7–10	800	170	1,600	10	50–200

	Copper (mg)	Iodine (mg)	Iron (mg)	Manganese (mcg)
0–6 mos.	0.4–0.6	40	6	0.3–0.6
6 mos.–1 yr.	0.6–0.7	50	10	0.6–1.0
0–1				
1–3	0.7–1.0	70	10	1.0–1.5
4–6	1.0–1.5	90	10	1.5–2.0
7–10	1.5–2.5	120	10	2.0–3.0

	Molybdenum (mcg)	Selenium (mcg)	Phosphorus (mg)	Sodium (mg)
0–6 mos.	15–30	10	300	120
6 mos.–1 yr.	20–40	15	500	200
0–1				
1–3	25–50	20	800	225
4–6	30–75	20	800	300
7–10	50–150	30	800	400–500

Sources: *Encyclopedia of Nutritional Supplements* by Michael T. Murray, N.D., and *Smart Medicine for a Healthier Child* by Janet Zand, L.Ac., O.M.D., Rachel Walton, R.N., Bob Rountree, M.D.

Appendix A

A Child's Materia Medica⋆
A Parent's Natural Home Pharmacy

This appendix will help you decide what to include in your home's natural pharmacy. Besides basic medical supplies such as bandages and hot-water bottles, it discusses the basic aromatherapy, herbal, homeopathic, and Bach Flower Remedies you may wish to have on hand to help treat common childhood complaints, illnesses, and minor injuries. Guidelines for determining age-appropriate dosages of herbal medicines and for preparing remedies with essential oils are also included.

Those upset stomachs, headaches, colds, coughs, flus, fevers, cuts, scrapes, and bee stings always seem to occur after doctor's office hours or on weekends. But, for most common childhood ills, a parent's loving administration of the appropriate natural remedy is the best therapy. Just having these supplies on hand—plus the emergency phone numbers for your family doctor and hospital—will give you peace of mind. When the next emergency strikes, you'll be better prepared mentally as well as materially to deal with it calmly and effectively.

When your child turns to you for care and comfort, your calm and loving response can immediately start the healing process. In fact, a special cup of herbal tea, a warm lavender or eucalyptus-scented bath, a cool chamomile compress accompanied by your soothing presence and the reading of an

---

⋆By contributing author Lara Pizzorno, M.A. (Div.), M.A. (Lit.), L.M.T.

extra bedtime story—such healing moments may remain among your son's or daughter's fondest, most cherished memories of childhood.

This section provides a brief introduction to the principles behind the four natural therapeutic modalities—aromatherapy, homeopathy, herbal medicine, and Bach Flower Remedies—from which the medicines in your natural home pharmacy are derived. The description of each type of therapy is followed by a listing of its most frequently used medicines, plus a brief description of their most common uses.

AROMATHERAPY

Although the use of aromatic oils to promote health and well-being dates back to the time of Hippocrates, the father of medicine (circa 4000 B.C.), the scientific study of their therapeutic properties began in France in the early 1920s. A cosmetic chemist, René-Maurice Gatefosse, burned his arm badly one day while making fragrances. He thrust the burned arm into the nearest cold liquid—a tub of lavender oil. To his surprise, the pain almost immediately dissipated, and the burn healed very quickly without leaving a scar and without developing any of the normal burn reactions of redness, heat, inflammation, and blisters. Gattefosse, who later coined the term *aromatherapy*, dedicated the rest of his life to researching the healing properties of essential oils.

Modern research has now confirmed centuries of practical use, demonstrating that various aromatic oils are antiviral, antibacterial, antifungal, antiseptic, anti-inflammatory, antidepressant, analgesic, and diuretic. In addition, essential oils can be used to enhance circulation, digestion, expectoration, and much more. Plants are chemical factories, combining the sun's energy with the earth's minerals in the presence of water and air to create fuel for life and growth. A plant's essential oil is its highest-grade super octane, containing, on average, a hundred biologically active components, including terpenes, alcohols, esters, aldehydes, ketones, and phenols. The aromatic chemicals in essential oils derive from phenylpropane and are precursors of the amino acids our bodies use to create and rebuild everything from enzymes to organs to skin and bones. Other chemicals in essential oils, the terpinols, derive from acetyl-coenzyme A, a molecule that plays an essential role in the production of hormones, vitamins, and energy.

For best therapeutic effect, use only pure essential oils—natural plant essences extracted by steam distillation or other natural methods. Products that are reconstituted or are chemical copies of natural essences—the so-called nature identicals, isolates, aromas, and perfume compounds—may smell delightful but are not medicinally effective. Check the label or try putting a drop of the essential oil on a piece of blotting paper. A pure essential oil evaporates and disperses, leaving no oily stain. Stored in tightly capped, dark-colored glass bottles away from light, heat, and dampness, essential oils will remain therapeutically active for about two years.

Methods of Application of Essential Oils

1. Apply 1 drop to a cotton ball, tissue, or handkerchief. Sniff as needed.

2. Inhale as a vapor. Pour hot water into a bowl and add 2 or 3 drops of oil. Drape a towel over your head to form a tent. Lean over the bowl, keeping your eyes closed and your face about 10 inches away. Breathe deeply through your nose for about one minute. Or close the room's doors and windows, pour boiling water into a bowl, and add up to 9 drops of essential oil. In about five minutes, the aromatic chemicals will permeate the room.

3. Make a massage oil. Into a brown glass bottle, put 2 to 5 drops of essential oil per teaspoon of cold-pressed, organic vegetable oil. Turn the bottle upside down a few times, then roll briskly between your hands to disperse the essential oil. Cap tightly and store, preferably in the refrigerator, but at least in a cool, dry place. (Refrigerator storage is recommended due to the vegetable oil, which can easily turn rancid, not the essential oil, which is much more stable.) One-half teaspoon of massage oil is adequate for most children; 1 teaspoon will suffice for most adults.

4. In the bath, add a maximum of 8 drops to a warm bath. Soak for at least ten minutes.

5. In the shower, wash first, then add 2 to 4 drops of essential oil to a washcloth and rub briskly over the body while remaining under the running water and breathing in the aromatic steam.

6. Add 1 to 8 drops to your humidifier's water reservoir.

7. Make an air spray. Pour 1 cup warm water (filtered or distilled if possible) into a new spray bottle, add 4 drops of essential oil, shake to mix, and spray.

A Child's Basic Essential Oils

CHAMOMILE

Among its beneficial properties, chamomile is a gentle yet effective antibacterial, antiseptic, and disinfectant oil. For children, chamomile Roman is most valued for its calming actions, while chamomile German is the variety preferred for anti-inflammatory activity. Chamomile soothes nerves and can help a teething, anxious, or keyed-up child get to sleep. It is also soothing and healing in inflammatory conditions such as chickenpox, diaper rash, eczema, sties, burns, sunburns, insect bites, and fever.

Use any of the methods of application listed above. Baths and foot and back massages with chamomile Roman work best for insomnia. Massage oil also can be directly applied to diaper rash, eczema, burns, sunburns, and insect bites. Cool compresses work well for sties, rashes, insect bites, and fever. For chickenpox, add 10 drops chamomile German and 10 drops lavender to a bottle of calamine lotion, shake well, and apply all over the body twice daily. For bee and hornet stings, place a drop of neat (undiluted) chamomile German on a cold compress and apply directly to the sting three times a day for two days. For wasp stings, mix 2 drops chamomile German, 2 drops lavender, and 1 teaspoon cider vinegar, and dab directly on the bite three times a day.

CLOVE

Best known for providing quick relief for toothache, clove oil is also an excellent remedy for sore, stiff muscles.

Do not use neat (undiluted) clove oil on the skin; clove oil is so powerful, it has been used to sterilize surgical instruments. Add clove oil to a warm bath or make a massage oil as directed above in methods of application and gently massage sore muscles. For a toothache, put a few drops of clove-infused oil on a cotton ball, or swab and apply directly to inflamed gums.

DILL

Dill is the oil of choice for infant colic and often relieves an older child's stomachache, too. For colic, dilute 1 drop of dill in 1 tablespoon sweet almond oil, and use to massage the baby's tummy with gentle, clockwise circles; then turn the baby over and use the same gentle circular pattern on the middle of the back. For older children, add 9 drops dill and 2 drops geranium to 2 tablespoons vegetable oil, and massage tummy and back in a clockwise direction.

EUCALYPTUS

A truly essential oil for colds, coughs, flu, or seasonal allergy—anytime your child is congested—eucalyptus is anti-inflammatory, antiseptic, antibiotic, and analgesic. Its cooling properties can soothe a sunburn, while the chemicals that give eucalyptus its cleansing aroma make it an effective insect repellent. The best eucalyptus oil, if you can find it, is *Eucalyptus radiata*.

Use any of the methods of application listed above. For sunburn, cool compresses or a lukewarm bath are the best choices. For congestion, a shower rub with a eucaplytus-treated washcloth provides immediate relief. Rubbing some massage oil on your child's chest and back or adding eucalyptus to your humidifier's water reservoir soothes and heals. To use eucalyptus as an insect repellent, dab some eucalyptus massage oil behind ears and on elbows, back, chest, and knees.

GERANIUM

Its delightful floral fragrance, combined with its sedative, astringent, and antiseptic properties, makes geranium excellent for fretfulness or insomnia, stomachaches, constipation, or diarrhea.

Add geranium to a warm bath, or use in massage oil for a foot rub to soothe your child to sleep. A gentle clockwise tummy massage can provide relief for digestive and eliminative complaints.

LAVENDER

A truly indispensable oil, lavender is a powerful antiseptic, antibiotic, antidepressant, and sedative. Its use on cuts, scrapes, and burns speeds healing and prevents scarring. Its calming properties allay the shock of injury—one deep breath of its miraculous scent and tension flows away.

Apply neat (undiluted) lavender to burns. Or place 2 drops on a clean washcloth, wring it out in a bowl of ice water, and apply as a cold compress. For bites from bees, wasps, gnats, and mosquitoes, apply several drops of neat undiluted lavender directly to the area three times a day. For ticks, a drop of thyme linalol placed directly on the tick's body will make it drop off; then apply a drop of lavender neat undiluted; wait five minutes and apply another drop to avoid infection and reduce pain and swelling. Use lavender in baths or massage oil for insomnia and in massage oil for tummyaches. For fevers, soak a cloth in a bowl of lukewarm water to make a compress, and apply to forehead, armpits, and lower back. For swollen glands that often accompany a sore throat or earache, combine 1 drop each of lavender, eucalyptus, and tea tree oil, mix these combined oils into 1 teaspoon of vegetable oil, and rub gently into the swollen areas; or use this combination of oils on a warm compress and apply over the throat area.

LEMON

Lemon is another good antiseptic for cuts, scrapes, and sore throats and is also an effective antiviral agent against warts.

For cuts and scrapes, add 10 drops to a pint of warm water and use as a cleansing solution. Dry and cover with a bandage on which you've put 1 drop of lavender. Mix the following gargle for a child older than one year with a sore throat: combine 3 tablespoons cider vinegar, 1 tablespoon honey, 3 drops ginger, and 5 drops lemon, and blend well. Put 1 teaspoon in a glass of warm water and gargle twice daily. (The child must be older than one year due to the presence of honey in this formula; honey can cause infant botulism in children less than one year old. For children less than one year old, substitute just enough rice syrup or maple syrup to render the gargle palatable.) Warts are caused by viruses and can be effectively treated using a combination of 10 drops lemon oil plus 5 drops lavender oil diluted in 2 teaspoons of cider vinegar. Mix well and apply directly to the wart twice daily using a cotton swab or cotton ball. Be careful to get the oil only on the wart and not on the surrounding skin.

PEPPERMINT

An excellent carminative or digestive aid, peppermint can help heal your child's indigestion, flatulence, bad breath, and headaches due to excessive food consumption or eating a food that doesn't agree with him.

For tummyaches and flatulence, add 15 drops peppermint oil to 2 table-spoons vegetable oil and gently massage the tummy and back in a clockwise motion. For bad breath, dilute 4 drops peppermint in 1 teaspoon glycerin, add to a glass of warm water, and use as a mouthwash. For headaches whose cause is unknown, combine 1 drop peppermint and 3 drops lavender; blend with 1 drop vegetable oil and massage around temples, base of skull, and hairline. Diarrhea and gastric-related headaches in children older than one year can be eased by sipping a mixture of 1 drop peppermint oil with 1 teaspoon of honey dissolved in warm water. (For children younger than one year, substitute maple syrup.)

ROSEMARY

A physical and mental stimulant, rosemary is the oil to use for a morning shower or bath on the day of an important school test. Rosemary's invigorating properties make it an excellent oil for cleansing away the aches and pains of muscular-related complaints—sore, fatigued muscles, and sprains and strains. Constipation and tummyaches also respond well to rosemary. Head lice hate the aromatic chemicals in rosemary, so this essential oil is an excellent preventive against lice infestation or eliminative agent should lice become established.

When your child's muscles are sore from too much exercise, the following massage oil formula will work wonders. Combine 5 drops rosemary, 5 drops lavender, and 5 drops peppermint in 2 tablespoons vegetable oil. For tummyaches and constipation, mix 15 drops rosemary with 2 tablespoons vegetable oil and use to massage tummy and back in a clockwise motion. To protect against lice, combine 5 drops each rosemary, lavender, and lemon, mix well, and add 2 drops of this mix to the final rinse after shampooing. If your child already has head lice, remember that infection is not due to poor hygiene; lice can jump from one child's cap or jacket to another's or from one head to another on a crowded school bus. To help get rid of a lice infestation, rub the following remedy into the scalp and leave it on overnight. Combine 27 drops each of rosemary, geranium, and lavender. Combine 1 ounce beeswax (melted in a double boiler) and 2 ounces castor oil, and stir to a creamy consistency. Let cool, then mix in the essential oils, stirring well.

TEA TREE

The most powerful antiseptic of all essential oils, tea tree is an impressive antiviral, antibacterial, and antifungal effective in treating all sorts of infections, including athlete's foot, coughs and colds, earaches, fever, flu, mumps, measles, and ringworm.

For athlete's foot, give your child a foot bath composed of 5 drops tea tree and 1 cup rock salt in a large bowl of water. Soak feet for at least five minutes daily. Dry feet thoroughly, then dust with a foot powder made by adding 10 drops tea tree to 1 cup green clay or aluminum-free talc. Wear only cotton or wool socks. Avoid nylon socks, which will hold in perspiration. Before bed, dip a cotton swab in a therapeutic oil made from 5 drops tea tree, 1 drop lemon, and 1 teaspoon vegetable oil, and apply between toes and around nails. Treat coughs and colds using the following synergistic blend: 10 drops each tea tree, eucalyptus, and lavender. For an ear infection, warm 1 teaspoon olive oil and add 3 drops tea tree and 1 drop lavender; blend well. Use this mixture as a massage oil, or soak a piece of cotton in it and use as an ear plug. For flu, add 5 drops tea tree, 2 drops lavender, and 2 drops thyme linalol to a warm bath; after the bath, massage your child's whole body with an oil made from 2 drops tea tree and 3 drops eucalyptus diluted in 1 teaspoon vegetable oil. For swollen glands, use this blend of 2 drops tea tree and 3 drops eucalyptus diluted in 1 teaspoon vegetable oil on a lukewarm compress applied to the swollen area. To cool a fever, add 10 drops of this same blend to a bowl of lukewarm water; immerse a compress, wring it out, and apply to forehead, armpits, tummy, and back. As soon as the compress warms up, exchange it for a cooler one. For mumps and measles, add 4 drops tea tree to 1 pint of water and use this solution to sponge down your child once a day. You can also use this mixture of 4 drops tea tree to 1 pint of water in a humidifier or air spray bottle. Diffused in the air, this essential oil will help not only to heal your child but also to protect others from contracting these infections.

Tea tree oil is especially effective against ringworm. Apply 1 neat undiluted drop directly to the infected area three times a day; the infection should clear completely within ten days. After the infection has cleared, follow up with an oil composed of 30 drops tea tree in 2 tablespoons vegetable oil. One caution: For those with sensitive skin, undiluted tea tree may be irritating if applied neat undiluted. Use a foot soak or medicinal oil application instead.

THYME LINALOL

Thyme linalol, a species of thyme usually grown at high altitudes, is slightly more expensive but is the only species that should be used for children. Thyme is a powerful antiviral and should never be applied to the skin undiluted; however, used properly, it is safe and extremely effective for a wide range of conditions, including bronchitis, flu, warts, and whooping cough.

Use thyme linalol in a humidifier or spray bottle, add 2 to 5 drops to a warm bath, or dilute 2 drops in 1 teaspoon of vegetable oil. Spray thyme linalol around door and screen frames and in under counter cabinets, and you will also protect your home from parasites and insects.

HOMEOPATHY

Developed by a German medical doctor, Samuel Hahnemann (1755–1843), homeopathy is a precise system of pharmaceutical treatment that uses minute doses of natural plant, mineral, and animal substances to stimulate the body's own healing defenses. Seeking to understand the reason why *Cinchona officinalis* (Peruvian bark) was an effective treatment against malaria, Hahnemann rejected the conventional wisdom that cinchona cured because of its bitter and astringent properties. Other plants and botanical medicines were more bitter and astringent than cinchona but did nothing to help sufferers recover from malaria. One of the premier physicians of his day, Hahnemann decided to run a controlled experiment. He took cinchona himself and promptly developed all the symptoms of malaria. This experience led him to test numerous plants, chemicals, and minerals, first on himself, then on healthy volunteers. In each instance, he noted the same interesting effect: certain extracts produced symptoms similar to those produced by certain diseases.

The Law of Similars

As his experimentation evolved, Hahnemann noted that instead of causing symptoms, very minute doses of extracts would cure a person of the same symptoms a large dose would produce. From this phenomenon, he developed homeopathy's most fundamental principle, the law of similars: Like cures like. He coined the name *homeopathy* for the new medical science, creating the term from two Greek derivatives, *homeo,* meaning like or similar, and *pathos,* meaning disease or suffering.

Potentization

Hahnemann's research also uncovered an astounding fact that scientists are still trying to explain: The more diluted the remedy, the more powerfully it mobilizes the body's healing forces and the less doses are needed. Homeopathic medicines are made by diluting the plant, mineral, or animal substance in double distilled water—usually one part substance to nine parts water—and then vigorously shaking the solution. If this process is completed twelve times, the medicine's strength is 12X (X stands for the Roman numeral for 10). More powerful remedies are produced when a substance is diluted 1 part substance to 99 parts water; a remedy diluted like this twelve times would have a 12C potency (C stands for the Roman numeral 100). The majority of homeopathic medicines sold for household use are in the lower end of the X potencies, but the process of dilution may be repeated 3, 6, 12, 30, 200, 1,000, 10,000, or 50,000 times. Homeopathic physicians often use single-dose remedies at the 200C potency.

According to present laws of physics, when a substance has been diluted to 24X or 12C, in all probability no molecules of the original substance remain. Consequently, this principle—the smaller the dose, the more potent and deeper acting the medicine—has been very controversial, to say the least. Skeptics base their attacks on homeopathy on this concept, claiming any positive benefit must be due to placebo effect. Yet research has repeatedly demonstrated that homeopathic medicines produce statistically significant beneficial results not only in adults and children but also in infants and animals—two groups in which a placebo response is unlikely.

Individualization

A second important principle of homeopathic philosophy, individualization, can be summed up by this statement: It is more important to know what kind of person has a disease than to know what kind of disease a person has. Homeopathic medicines are based on the unique way the illness presents itself in the individual, rather than on the illness itself. Take the common cold, for example. One child may sneeze constantly; have lots of watery, burning, nasal discharge from both nostrils; watery eyes; have a red, irritated, tender nose; be restless and irritable; and want lots of cool water to drink.

Another may have thick yellow mucus, congestion that blocks up one side of the nose and then switches to the other, or a sore throat or a cough; be lethargic and clingy; and want acidic liquids like orange juice. Both children have a cold, but each one's pattern of symptoms is quite different.

The proper homeopathic medicine reflects your child's entire pattern of symptoms, including his mental and emotional state, not just the generic illness. When your child has a cold, she may become anxious and fretful, clingy and weepy, or irritable and want to be left alone. Her mental and emotional responses may vary, but reappear consistently as her typical response no matter what the ailment. As the overview of specific homeopathic remedies below clearly demonstrates, these elements of your child's personal response to illness are not only considered, they are also important factors in the choice of the appropriate homeopathic remedy. In fact, recurrent body-mind patterns, which include the physical, mental, and emotional symptoms a person habitually exhibits, make up what homeopaths describe as a constitutional type. The remedy that best helps the body bring this constellation of symptoms into a healthy balance is called a *constitutional remedy*. Knowing your child's constitutional remedy is effective in treating both acute and chronic symptoms and enables you to better understand and help your child.

Since Hahnemann's day, literally millions of experiments (called *provings* in homeopathic jargon) have been done on hundreds of plant, mineral, and animal substances, and the results checked and rechecked thousands of times and recorded in homeopathic resource books called a repertory and a materia medica. A *repertory* contains lists of every imaginable symptom—mental and emotional as well as physical—along with the homeopathic medicines known to cure it. *Materia medica* is Latin for "materials of medicine," and this resource contains a list of homeopathic medicines, each followed by a description of the symptoms it is known to treat. Not surprisingly, these resources are both detailed and complex. If you are merely searching for a remedy to help your child deal with a minor complaint, you will likely be successful consulting the brief repertory in this appendix or the Parent's Natural Home Health Kit in Appendix B. If you wish to determine your child's constitutional remedy, you may wish to consult with a homeopathic physician (see Finding a Competent Homeopathic Physician, below).

Homeopathy Today

Today homeopathic medicine is widely practiced in Europe. England's royal family has been under homeopathic care since the 1830s, and 42 percent of British physicians refer patients to homeopaths. One-third of the French population uses homeopathic medicines; 32 percent of French physicians prescribe them. One-fifth of all German physicians and 45 percent of Dutch physicians consider homeopathic medicines effective.

State-of-the-art scientific research on homeopathic medicines continues to demonstrate their effectiveness. In the September 20, 1997, issue of *The Lancet,* a highly respected medical journal, a team of German and American physicians and scientists published a review of eighty-nine clinical studies evaluating the efficacy of homeopathic remedies. These studies covered a wide variety of ailments, including asthma, hay fever, ear infection, upper respiratory infection, influenza, migraine headache, rheumatoid arthritis, sprains and strains, diarrhea, indigestion, postsurgical complications, varicose veins, and childbirth. The results? Patients given a homeopathic remedy were 2.45 times more likely to have a positive result than those given a placebo.

Finding a Competent Homeopathic Physician

Many N.D.s (naturopathic doctors) and other holistically oriented physicians utilize homeopathy. To find a physician or other health care practitioner who specializes in homeopathy, check with the following national organizations for a list of qualified homeopaths in your area:

Homeopathic Educational Service
2124 Kittredge St.
Berkeley, CA 94704
Telephone: (415) 649-0294

International Foundation for Homeopathy
2366 Eastlake Ave. E, Suite 301
Seattle, WA 98102
Telephone: (206) 324-8230

National Center of Homeopathy
1500 Massachusetts Ave. NW, #42
Washington, DC 20005
Telephone: (202) 223-6182

How to Take Homeopathic Medicines

Homeopathic medicines are usually in the form of small, white medicated pellets, most often in a lactose (milk sugar) or sucrose base. The pellets come in different sizes (#10 looks like tiny confectioner's sprinkles; #35 looks like a white version of the little silver balls used to decorate holiday cookies and cakes; others look like small aspirin tablets). Dosage normally is on the bottle label, but, in general, dosages are 5–10 cake sprinkles, 2–4 spherical balls, or 1–2 tablets.

Store homeopathic medicines in a cool, dark place, away from strong odors (camphor, eucalyptus, perfume, etc.), and away from electromagnetic fields (heating pads, electric blankets, microwaves, computers, televisions). Do not refrigerate.

To take the remedy, tap the appropriate number of pellets into the cap of the bottle, then pour the pellets *directly* into the child's mouth, under her tongue. Do not place the pellets in your hand or in any other container first. The remedy should be allowed to dissolve slowly under the tongue, although it will probably still work if it is chewed. No food (even chewing gum) or drink should be taken thirty minutes before or after a dose, and no strong odors, such as those from toothpaste, mouthwash, or throat lozenges, should be in the child's mouth—it should be empty and naturally clean.

The following also should be avoided, as they may interfere with or antidote a homeopathic remedy:

- *Coffee*—even decaffeinated coffee sometimes interferes with remedies. Chances are your young child is not a coffee drinker, but your teenager may be and should avoid it, especially if he is sensitive to its influence.

- *Highly aromatic substances*—camphor, eucalyptus, Ben-Gay, Vicks, Noxzema, Tiger Balm, deep-heating rubs, liniments, and cough lozenges should be avoided.

- *Drugs*—both prescription and over-the-counter drugs are designed to take over various bodily functions and block or mask symptoms, whereas homeopathic remedies work by encouraging the body's healing response. Medicinal herbs and large doses of vitamins also should be avoided.

- *Dental work*—drilling and anesthetics interfere.

- *Electric blankets and heating pads*—these create an electromagnetic effect that sometimes interferes.

Homeopathic Medicines

The following twenty-five remedies provide you with homeopathic alternatives for most any common childhood ailment.

1. Aconitum
2. *Allium cepa*
3. *Anas barbariae* (marketed under the name *Oscillococcinum*)
4. *Apis mellifica*
5. *Arnica montana*
6. *Arsenicum album*
7. Belladonna
8. *Bryonia alba*
9. *Calcarea carbonica*
10. Cantharis
11. Chamomilla
12. Euphrasia
13. Gelsemium
14. Hypericum
15. Ignatia
16. *Kali bichromicum*
17. *Ledum palustre*
18. *Magnesia phosphorica*
19. Mercurius
20. *Natrum muriaticum*
21. *Nux vomica*
22. Pulsatilla
23. *Rhus toxicodendron*

24. *Ruta graveolens*

25. Sulphur

Homeopathic Combination Medicines

Typically, three to eight homeopathic medicines that are effective in treating a particular condition are combined in these user-friendly medicines. While not as individualized, they still can be effective and also will eliminate the need to switch from a remedy used in the initial stages of a complaint (like Aconite or Arnica) to remedies that continue the healing process (like *Rhus tox,* Hypericum, or Ruta).

In addition to the flu remedy mentioned above, Oscillococcinum, three other combination remedies to have on hand are:

- *Similisan*—homeopathic eye drops good for any ailment that irritates the eyes.

- *Traumeel*—a homeopathic cream that will help heal all types of bumps, bruises, sprains, and strains, but should not be applied to open wounds.

- If your child is susceptible to coughs, a good combination remedy to have on hand is *Boericke & Tafel Sugar-free Herbal Cough and Bronchial Syrup,* which helps relieve coughs, loosen phlegm, and thin bronchial secretions.

A Brief Repertory of Children's Basic Homeopathic Remedies

This section discusses each remedy's general uses and *modalities*—those factors commonly recognized as either aggravating or providing relief for the child who needs this particular remedy. Modalities provide further clues that a certain remedy is the correct choice.

ACONITUM (Aconite)

General uses: The vitamin C of homeopathy, aconite is indicated at the first stages of many infectious diseases with sudden, often intense onset of symptoms including fever, acute inflammation, and shock from injury or surgery. Common complaints for which aconite may be helpful include the common cold, influenza, sore throat, cough, laryngitis, cystitis (bladder infection), earache, chickenpox, German measles, measles, mumps, black eye, toothache, shock from injury or surgery (use aconite pre- and postsurgery). Aconitum is useful not for chronic or recurring symptoms, but for symptoms that come on quickly, usually after exposure to cold, dry weather, or extremely hot weather (such weather extremes stress a child's immune system, lowering immune resistance and increasing susceptibility to a virus or bacteria).

Modalities: The child who will benefit most from aconitum will be hot, dry, anxious, restless, and irritable. He may be fearful or have a feeling of foreboding. He will typically be thirsty, usually for cold drinks, and will have difficulty falling asleep because his symptoms will be worse at night. He'll feel worse in dry, cold wind; warm rooms; in the evening and night; or lying on the affected side. He'll feel better in open air, after perspiring, and when sitting still.

ALLIUM CEPA (red onion)

General uses: Alllium cepa is the remedy when your child has a cold with symptoms of clear, burning, nasal discharge; reddened nostrils and upper lip; watery eyes with a bland discharge; and sneezing. This remedy is also frequently helpful for hay fever and other respiratory allergies, earache, and laryngitis. If your child's nasal discharge is bland but the discharge from his eyes is irritating, see Euphrasia.

Modalities: Further clues that your child will benefit from *Allium cepa* are that he feels worse in warm rooms, from getting wet, or in cold, damp winds; open air and cool rooms make him feel better.

ANAS BARBARIAE (heart and liver of a duck)

General uses: Marketed under the name *Oscillococcinum,* this is the most popular flu remedy in France. Eighty percent of ducks carry every known influenza virus in their digestive tracts, so *Anas barb* can be thought of as the homeopathic equivalent of chicken soup. Oscilloccinum works best during the initial onset of flu (the first 48 hours) with symptoms of fever, body aches, general weakness, and a runny nose or cough.

Modalities: No widely recognized individualizing symptoms. *Anas barb* is considered a generic flu remedy.

APIS MELLIFICA (common name: crushed bee)

General uses: Bee venom contains a protein that provokes a histamine reaction, and the sting results in a bright red swelling that is very sensitive to the touch. Apis is the remedy for grass and pollen allergies or any ailment where the primary symptoms include swelling with burning, stinging pain such as hives, insect bites, bee stings, chickenpox, measles, conjuctivitis, sore throat, and sties.

Modalities: The child who will benefit most from apis is easily irritated, fidgety, and clumsy. She is hypersensitive and cannot bear the slightest touch on the inflamed part. Her mouth is dry. Her discomfort is aggravated by heat, and she may feel worse around 3 P.M. She feels better when sitting up, uncovered, in cool air, with the application of cool compresses or after a cool bath.

ARNICA MONTANA (Arnica)

General uses: Arnica is the remedy to use as first aid in common injuries, sprains and strains, or the stiffness, aches, and pains that follow heavy exercise. Arnica helps normalize heart activity after injury, thus stopping hemorrhage, and helps the body reabsorb blood clots and the blood pooling under the skin that causes hematomas (black-and-blue marks). Arnica stimulates the repair of bruised and damaged blood vessels, and reduces pain and swelling. It is effective in treating ruptures of the tiny blood vessels that appear in the whites of the eye after injury as well as black eyes, and is used before and after surgery to lessen shock, relieve pain and swelling, and promote healing. Should your child undergo circumcision; suffer a fracture, sprain, or strain; or have his fingers or toes caught in a door, give Arnica! Taken before and after strenuous exercise, arnica will help prevent muscle aches and stiffness. For muscle aches, sprains, and strains, using both arnica tablets and gently massaging in a gel or ointment will help; for injuries where the skin is broken, or for head injuries, use only internal doses of Arnica.

Modalities: The child who will benefit from arnica will feel bruised and tender, achy, stiff, and most likely exhausted. He will feel better lying down with the windows open to let in fresh air, but worse from motion, exertion, touch, cold, or heat.

ARSENICUM ALBUM (white arsenic)

General uses: Arsenicum is often the best remedy when a cold, sinusitis, sore throat, cough, flu, allergy, or asthma attack begins after your child has been chilled, or when symptoms of exhaustion appear after completing a major achievement. Arsenicum is also useful against conjunctivitis, diarrhea, indigestion, food poisoning, fever, headaches, nervous restlessness, insomnia, and impetigo.

Modalities: When your child awakens at or after midnight and comes to you with chills, a fever, headache, difficulty breathing, or a digestive problem, turn to arsenicum. Your child may have burning pains in the head, throat, stomach, bladder, or vagina; burning discharges from the eyes, nose, or vagina; or a burning sensation when urinating or defecating. Although the discomfort is a burning one, heat and warm compresses provide relief. She will typically have a dry mouth and be very thirsty, but be able to take only frequent small sips of lukewarm water. Cold food and drinks, especially milk, ice cream, melon, strawberries, and other fruits will make her feel worse, while warm food and drinks will be soothing. Children who benefit most from arsenicum are frequently restless, high strung, fastidious, sensitive to noise, and easily frightened. Their vivid imaginations conjure fears, so being alone in the dark is scary. Anxious about their health, they fear they are more ill than they appear. This child likes attention, desires company, and truly may feel much weaker and more exhausted than would be expected. Being both fussy and a perfectionist, he may insist on cleaning up his room even though he feels quite ill.

BELLADONNA (deadly nightshade)

General uses: The name *belladonna* derives from the Italian words *bella,* "beautiful," and *donna,* "woman." The plant was so named because one of its primary chemical components, atropine, causes the pupils to dilate, resulting in the large pupils regarded as beautiful in ancient times. In addition to atropine, belladonna contains other powerful alkaloids, including hyoscyamine and scopolamine, which affect the autonomic nervous system, that part of the nervous system that controls involuntary bodily functions such as digestion, circulation, and reproductive cycles. Consider using belladonna when the ailment is accompanied by an intense throbbing or stabbing pain that suddenly appears and disappears. Headaches; cramps; colic; toothaches; sore throats; earaches; fevers, if of sudden onset and accompanied by throbbing, stabbing pains, may be relieved by belladonna. Belladonna also may help a child with chickenpox if the rash is accompanied by a severe headache, flushed face, and hot skin. Belladonna acts quickly—improvement is usually seen within an hour and often within fifteen minutes.

Modalities: The face and mucous membranes of the child who will be aided by belladonna are dry, red, and hot. He is hypersensitive to and aggravated by cold air, light, touch, being jarred, motion, noise, and lying down. Painful symptoms are usually worse on the right side, and worse at night, especially after midnight. Helpful factors are sitting up and resting in a warm, dimly lit room.

BRYONIA ALBA (wild hops)

General uses: Distinct from aconitum or belladonna, both of which help children with sudden onset of symptoms, bryonia is useful when symptoms come on more slowly. Your child may develop a cold after getting chilled or after gulping a cold drink when he is overheated. Over the next few days, the cold will evolve into a painful cough with congestion, headache, and fever accompanied by indigestion, constipation, even pneumonia. The child's mouth and lips will be dry, and his tongue dry and white coated. He'll be constantly thirsty, requesting cold drinks. Digestive juices will dry up, too, causing lack of appetite, trouble digesting what is eaten, and constipation with dry, hard, large stools.

Modalities: The child needing bryonia will be grumpy, peevish, and irritable, asking for something and then not wanting it, wishing to be left alone in a dark, cool room, quiet and motionless because any movement aggravates his symptoms. He may hold his head when he talks, or hold his chest when he coughs. His discomfort will be aggravated by dry heat, warm rooms, and any movement. Even carrying this child to bed makes symptoms worse. He'll try to lie on the part that feels painful, since pressure helps, but he won't want to be touched. He'll feel better with cool drinks and cold food, if his appetite permits.

CALCAREA CARBONICA (calcium carbonate)

General uses: Calcarea carbonica is usually given based more on the child's normal characteristics than on the symptoms of an illness, though the calcarea child frequently suffers from a runny nose, earaches, distended abdomen, colic, diaper rash, diarrhea alternating with constipation, and sour-smelling breath, perspiration, and stools. These children are often allergic to cow's milk and react with indigestion or other symptoms after drinking it.

Modalities: Most often, the child who needs calcarea is pudgy or, at least, has flabby skin tone. She's stubborn, prefers to move slowly if at all, and tends to avoid either physical or mental effort because she hates being teased or criticized for doing things slowly. Though slow, this child can be very bright but just needs to do things at her own pace. When left to her own devices, the calcarea child will be complacent and happy playing quietly by herself. But calcarea children are fearful—of the dark, insects, animals, heights, new challenges, her own scary dreams—and therefore clingy. Her head and feet will sweat profusely, especially at night or from even slight exertion. These children don't do well in cold weather and tend to get recurrent infections (colds, coughs, earaches, sore throats) during the winter. They crave soft-boiled eggs, breads, pasta, potatoes, ice cream, sweets, and cold drinks. Finally, a definite sign that your child would benefit from calcarea is a craving for indigestible items like dirt, chalk, and coal.

CANTHARIS (Spanish fly)

General uses: Cantharis is the remedy to use for bladder infection or similar symptoms in the urinary tract, lower bowel, and skin, including blisters and burns. If your child has a burning, cutting pain while urinating, urgency and constant desire to urinate, yet an inability to urinate more than a few drops, cantharis will help. A child needing cantharis may feel burning pain in various places—head, eyes, throat, stomach, intestinal tract, ovaries. She may feel as if she is on fire inside but may have chills on the outside, and she may be thirsty but not want to drink. Her discomfort will make her hypersensitive and restless, frequently changing positions in her sleep or unable to sleep well at night.

Modalities: The child who will benefit from cantharis will feel worse before, during, and after urination and after drinking fluids. She'll also be restless and sensitive to touch or motion. If she can belch or pass gas, it will help. So will both cold and warm applications; cooling baths or applications soothe burning, while warmth will help with her chills.

CHAMOMILLA (chamomile)

General uses: Chamomilla, renowned for its soothing effect, is often given to teething infants whose normal sweet and happy demeanor has given way to inconsolable irritability or an out-and-out tantrum because they are so uncomfortable. In any illness when a normally nice child turns into a tempermental, hyperrestless monster, it's time to give chamomilla. Common ailments in which chamomilla may prove useful include anger, asthma, colic, diarrhea, earache, indigestion, insomnia, restlessness, teething, and toothache.

Modalities: The child who needs chamomilla often will have a distinctive appearance. She will look inflamed, but one cheek will be red and hot while the other is pale and cold. Her head may be warm and moist with sweat; her feet hot and dry and irritated by being under the bedcovers. In addition to a sour disposition, she may have sour-smelling stools, breath, body odor, or gas. If a tantrum is on the way, it will most likely occur either mid-morning or mid-evening (9 A.M. or 9 P.M.). Being carried or being driven in a car may help her feel better, but heat, wind, and touch will aggravate her symptoms.

EUPHRASIA (eyebright)

General uses: The homeopathic treatment for children with hay fever or other allergies with itchy, burning, watery, tearing eyes. The child's eyes may feel as if grit or pepper has gotten into them. The edges of the eyelids may be red, swollen, and burning. The discomfort will cause the child to blink often and scratch and rub his eyes. Upon waking in the morning, the eyelids may be gummed together. The child may be sensitive to light. Concurrent symptoms include clear, nonirritating, nasal discharge that is worse in the morning and when the child is outside; a productive cough; and a headache. The child will feel chilled and have difficulty warming up in bed.

Modalities: The child who will benefit most from euphrasia will feel worse in the morning, in cold air, windy weather, or bright light, but better in dimly light rooms or in the dark.

GELSEMIUM (yellow jasmine)

General uses: For a fatigued, drowsy-looking, glassy-eyed child who is anxious or has a cold, headache, flu, or measles. Her whole body, especially her limbs, may feel weak and heavy. Lips tend to be dry and cracked. She may tremble from chills, her face and head hot, while her extremities are cold. In contrast to aconitum and belladonna, symptoms come on gradually instead of suddenly. The child who will be relieved by gelsemium may have diarrhea or a headache from anxious anticipation of an exam, sports game, or performance. Although she may have a fever and her lips may be dry, she won't be thirsty yet will need to urinate profusely and will feel better afterward.

Modalities: The child who needs gelsemium tends to be emotional and may become ill after hearing bad news or after a sudden fright. Her condition will worsen in humid or damp weather, fog, after exposure to the sun, and after 10 P.M. She'll feel better when warm, after urinating, and in fresh air.

HYPERICUM (St. John's wort)

General uses: Hypericum stimulates the healing of injuries to nerves or areas of the body rich in nerves such as teeth, fingers, toes, spine, and head. The body signals us that nerve injury has occurred by producing shooting pains or numbness. Should your child slip and land on his tailbone, bite his tongue, receive a blow to the head, or have one of his front teeth knocked out or injured, start him on hypericum as soon as possible. As most surgery is traumatic for nerves, give hypericum at least once before surgery and afterward as needed. Hypericum is also used, both internally and externally, for treating puncture wounds from nails, splinters, pins, or animal bites or stings. Use calendula for superficial cuts and hypericum to help close deeper wounds. If using hypericum tincture externally, dilute it—10 parts water to 1 part tincture—or it will sting due to the tincture's alcohol content.

Modalities: Chosen according to type of wound rather than other symptoms. Your child will, however, feel better when lying still, and worse in cold or damp weather or before a storm.

IGNATIA (St. Ignatius bean)

General uses: A good choice for high-strung, sensitive, nervous, easily excitable children who often bottle up their anger, grief, or fear, pretending they are fine until finally exploding with rage or hysteria. Common presenting complaints are headache, indigestion, insomnia, and sore throat. The child who needs ignatia will sigh or yawn frequently, be easily upset or offended, and feel misunderstood. Ignatia is the remedy for children who have been physically or mentally abused. The child's moods fluctuate and are contradictory; she may be crying one second, laughing the next, or laughing through her tears. Her unexpressed emotions may feel stuck in her throat, and she may have a corresponding physical sensation of a lump in her throat or a lump in her stomach after eating. The ignatia child may tremble, have difficulty sleeping, and have a tendency to faint.

Modalities: Emotional upsets and repressing emotions—anxiety, grief, depression, anger—will increase discomfort. Warmth, an activity that takes the child's mind off her anxiety, gentle pressure on the painful part—all will ameliorate symptoms.

KALI BICHROMICUM (potassium bichromate)

General uses: Use *Kali bic* for allergies, colds, coughs, croup, headaches, laryngitis, measles, and sinusitis when your child is producing thick, stringy, gluey, lumpy yellow or greenish mucus from nose, eyes, throat, or chest. Other signs that *Kali bic* is the correct remedy include listlessness, symptoms that migrate from one part of the body to another (headache is replaced by stomachache or diarrhea), slow digestion (the food sits in the stomach, so the child feels worse after eating), nausea, a craving for acidic drinks (hot tea with lemon, orange juice), and chills.

Modalities: Respiratory problems that respond to *Kali bic* generally occur in spring and autumn. The child will feel worse in cold air or wind, wet weather, if uncovered, and upon awakening. Summer weather discourages these respiratory problems, as does warmth. Motion and firm pressure help alleviate symptoms.

LEDUM PALUSTRE (wild rosemary, marsh tea)

General uses: A remedy to try when pain from an animal bite, insect sting, injury, or inflammation is relieved by cold applications or bathing. Ledum is a primary remedy for puncture wounds that are inflamed and itchy, such as bites and stings from mosquitoes, bees, spiders, and rats. It is also an excellent remedy for inflammation such as that caused by poison ivy, oak, or sumac, and by bruised muscles and connective tissue. Ledum's effectiveness in healing smaller capillaries makes it the remedy to try for bruises to hands and feet and black eyes, especially if arnica has helped but not cured the condition. Ledum is also the remedy to use for long-lasting bruises. If started immediately, a combination of ledum taken internally and arnica applied topically can heal a black eye overnight.

Modalities: If ledum is your child's remedy, he will feel better with cold applications, cool baths, cool fresh air, and rest, but worse from motion, at night, and from heat—the heat of bedclothes, warm clothing, warm air.

MAGNESIA PHOSPHORICA (phosphate of magnesium)

General uses: Mag phos is a primary remedy for colic, muscle and menstrual cramps, backaches, or spasms relieved by heat and pressure. The child may feel relief by staying quiet, warmly covered, and doubling up in a fetal position. *Mag phos* also is used for cramps, stiffness, or numbness that occurs after prolonged use of certain muscles in writing, playing an instrument, playing a video game, or taking a long hike or bike ride. If the cramping is abdominal, as in colic, the abdomen may be bloated, but passing gas doesn't help.

Modalities: Cramps will be eased by heat, warm applications, warm drinks, curling up in a fetal position, or firm pressure. Cold air, cold applications, and cold drinks will make the child feel worse.

MERCURIUS (mercury)

General uses: Mercury is used when an acute condition—such as diarrhea, sore throat, earache, toothache, food poisoning, mumps, or conjunctivitis—seems to be evolving rather than dissipating. Chronic ear infections often respond well to mercury. Typically, the child will be weak, restless, and hypersensitive to hot and cold. She will salivate profusely, soaking her pillow while sleeping. She also will perspire a lot but won't feel better afterward, and will have a dry throat, an intense thirst for cold drinks, and a hunger for sweets. Her sweat, breath, urine, and stools will have an offensive odor; diarrhea may cause a burning sensation. If a cold is the problem, it will settle in the throat, and the lymph glands will be swollen.

Modalities: Changes in the weather and extremes in temperature will make the child feel worse, as will any exertion, touch, or pressure, and being in the open air. Often her condition will worsen at night. The child will feel better during the day, if she is able to settle down and rest.

NATRUM MURIATICUM

General uses: The child who will benefit most from *Natrum muriaticum* is a perfectionist. Usually sensitive, intelligent, attractive, well groomed, well behaved, and neat and tidy, this child is ambitious, hard on himself, and eager to achieve. He may get a headache after intense mental work, such as preparing an important school report. If he makes a mistake while writing or doing artwork, he will tear up the page in frustration and consider himself a total failure. He keeps his room neat and organized, evidence of his perfectionism. He may not want to share his things with a friend or sibling, not because he is selfish but because he is afraid they will be damaged. *Nat mur* children are sensitive and caring; they blame themselves when anything goes wrong. If their parents divorce, these children will be certain it is their fault.

Nat mur children love salt, are often thirsty, and typically pass hard, dry stools. They have difficulty falling asleep because their minds are busily thinking over the day's experiences, planning the next day, or trying to solve the riddle of Infinity. Even if tired, a *Nat mur* child may try to force himself to stay awake so he can keep thinking about things. While sleeping, *Nat mur* children's heads or whole bodies may perspire. When a *Nat mur* child develops a cold, he will often say the inside of his runny nose hurts or burns; he may have a sore between his nose and upper lip, and his lips may be dry and cracked. If your son fits this profile, is on the shy side, and is having problems with enuresis (bedwetting), *Nat mur* will definitely help. If your child frequently gets cold sores, has recurrent diarrhea, or comes down with German measles with symptoms including swollen glands, a sore throat, rash, and canker sores, consider *Natrum muriaticum*.

Modalities: Nat mur children are often lactose intolerant or do not like milk, slimy foods, and fat. Illnesses may be initiated or made worse by emotional upsets, especially grief. Eyes and skin are sensitive to sun exposure. Direct sunlight will cause these children to squint or to develop headaches and will aggravate skin eruptions. *Nat mur* children tend to be warm-blooded, so they feel better with fresh air, light bedclothes, warm or cool rather than hot baths, and cool drinks. The opposites exacerbate their discomfort.

NUX VOMICA (poison nut)

General uses: Homeopathic Prozac, *Nux vomica* is the remedy for children who are overly excitable, hyperactive, and driven. *Nux vomica* children (and adults) are competitive people who live in the fast lane, work hard, and expect everyone else to keep up. Their zeal is counterbalanced by anxiety, and they are often tense, which makes them irritable, critical, and impatient. If sick, this child wants to be cured *right now!* Despite feeling ill, his fastidiousness and desire for everything to be both accurate and in order will cause this child to maintain his room's neatness (it will already be well organized). Because his nervous system is on fast forward, the *Nux vomica* child is a light sleeper and sensitive to noise, odors, touch, music, food, and drugs. A dark, quiet room is essential for this child; he needs adequate sleep to recharge and will be irritable and prone to illness without it.

Although he craves spicy foods and fats, the *Nux vomica* child may become bloated and flatulent about an hour after eating—particularly after eating meat, milk, and cold foods, which also may provoke headaches and respiratory problems such as asthma, allergy symptoms, and congestion. In addition to indigestion, particularly after overindulgence, children who will benefit from *Nux vomica* may become constipated, unable to go to the bathroom despite frequently feeling as if they need to. If a headache accompanies the constipation, it will be worse in the morning, exacerbated by exertion, light, sun exposure, or coughing. Lots of nasal discharge during the day and congestion at night is also typical.

Modalities: Prolonged mental or emotional stress, too much spicy or fatty food, drug use (prescribed or recreational), inadequate sleep, cold or windy weather, noise, light when trying to sleep—all will exacerbate symptoms. A good night's rest—unbroken, deep sleep; firm pressure on areas that hurt; and avoiding meat, milk, and cold foods when ill will help.

PULSATILLA (windflower)

General uses: Pulsatilla is often prescribed based more on the child's personality than on a specific ailment. This child soaks up affection and can't seem to get enough; she hates to be alone. As an infant, she needed to be physically attached to her mother, carried in a baby sling or carrier, and cried whenever placed in her crib for a nap. She's emotional and sensitive, open to and influenced by those around her and her environment. Changeable and moody, she may be crying one minute, laughing the next. Easily hurt, she will cry softly if she is criticized, punished, or feels ignored but will quickly become sunny again when she receives the sympathy and attention she needs. Fearing abandonment, she may become clingy, whiny, and jealous of her parents' attention to her siblings. Because of her impressionable nature, a children's movie with scary scenes will keep her up at night. She'll always want a night light on and may still frequently appear in her parents' bedroom for hugs and reassurance. She'll need help choosing what clothes to wear to school, what game to play, what food to eat at a restaurant—just about any decision, big or small. Her physical symptoms—wandering pains that alternate on each side of the body—reflect her changeable nature: congestion or a runny nose that moves from one nostril to another, conjunctivitis, or a sty that vanishes from one eye and appears on the other, a cold that becomes a cough, a sore throat that metamorphoses into an earache, a headache that is replaced by a stomachache. She won't be thirsty, even if she has a fever.

Modalities: Symptoms may manifest after eating rich or fatty foods. Warm, stuffy rooms or being chilled will exacerbate symptoms. Fresh air, gentle motion, cool applications, cold food, lying on the side that hurts—and lots of attention and sympathy—will help her feel better.

RHUS TOXICODENDRON (poison ivy)

General uses: The two hallmark indications that a child will benefit from *Rhus tox* are: (1) he is restless, always moving around when awake, tossing and turning when asleep, and (2) the rusty-gate syndrome—upon awakening, he'll feel stiff and achy; initial movement will aggravate things, but continued motion will make him feel better. When he finally rests, however, the syndrome will repeat. He'll feel achy on initial movement, then gradually better with continued movement. His illness may begin after he gets chilled or wet, especially if he has been playing and is overheated. Cold, wet weather will make him chilly and uncomfortable. At night, symptoms will worsen—his restlessness will prevent him from getting good rest, and what rest he gets will provoke the rusty-gate syndrome. He's susceptible to herpes blisters on his lips, which may be dry and cracked. He'll ask for cold drinks, even though they make him feel more chilly and worsen cough symptoms. *Rhus tox* is the most common remedy for chickenpox; the rash will be accompanied by intense itching, especially at night, making the child very restless. If, even when well, your child frequently complains of sore muscles after exertion, consider *Rhus tox.*

Modalities: Overexertion, rest, and cold, wet weather aggravate symptoms, which typically worsen at night. Continued motion and warmth—warm covers, warm applications—ameliorate symptoms.

RUTA GRAVEOLENS (rue)

General uses: Rue is the remedy to use for injuries to the periosteum (bone covering), tendons, or ligaments, or for any bruise that takes a long time to heal and leaves a calcified, knotty lump. Injuries to the periosteum occur at the knees, elbows, and shins. In carpal tunnel syndrome—an increasingly common problem in children due to frequent and prolonged use of video games and computer keyboards—knotty lumps appear in the connective tissue at the wrist. Any inflammation of muscles due to overuse and repetitive motion may respond well to ruta (arnica works best on sudden injury; *Rhus tox* on injury with rusty-gate syndrome). As teeth are actually part of the body's bone mass, ruta is also very effective in reducing pain and speeding healing after dental surgery or after a child's braces are put on or adjusted.

Before and after surgery on joints (knee, elbow, wrist, teeth), give ruta. Sprains and strains that feel hot to the touch will respond well to both ruta and *Rhus tox,* as do tennis elbow and chronic knee injuries.

Modalities: Injuries that will respond to ruta will feel better with warm applications and worse when pressure is applied, for example, kneeling on the injured knee.

SULPHUR

General uses: Sulphur is a remedy frequently used with success when acute conditions such as colds, flus, coughs, and ear infections linger on. When a lingering condition is not the problem, sulphur is another remedy chosen more in relation to the personality of the child than to the ailment. If the following profile fits your child, try sulphur for most any common condition, including allergies, bedwetting, boils, fever, headaches, hives, impetigo, measles, poison ivy or oak, sore throats, or styes. Sulphur children are intelligent, frequently ask "Why?" and easily integrate new information. New facts and figures fascinate them; they can rattle off every sports statistic for the last twenty years. They love to talk, are very entertaining, and may end up spinning stories, both to keep talking and to get attention. They are pack-rats, selfish about their possessions and careless with the possessions of others. Messy and usually in need of a bath (which they won't want to take), these are the children whose clothes and toys are strewn all over the house or left at a friend's. (If male, they grow up to be the men who leave the cap off the toothpaste tube and the toilet seat up.) Despite their unending energy, sulphur children need to be reminded a dozen times to do their chores and will procrastinate until the last minute. Their constant burning of energy makes them both hot and hungry. They eat a lot (except for breakfast, which they sleep through); favorite foods include salty chips, pizza, chocolate, ice cream, and ice cold sodas. Their internal heat is evident in their coloring—a reddened face; reddened mucous membranes; red lips; red edges of eyelids, nostrils, and ears; dry skin; and hot feet. Already warm enough and typically sweaty, they dislike warm weather, warm rooms, warm clothing (especially wool), and bedcovers (which they usually kick off). If they have a fever, they won't have chills and will prefer to be uncovered.

Modalities: Sulphur children feel much better in open cool air, with cool applications (forget baths; they dislike them so much they will likely feel worse afterward) and cool drinks. Both heat and extreme cold will aggravate symptoms.

HERBAL MEDICINES

Herbs are plants used for medicinal purposes. Not only do 80 percent of the world's population depend on herbs to treat common ailments, but 30 percent of modern conventional drugs are derived from plants. Aspirin is based on salicylic acid, a component of white willow bark and meadowsweet. As noted earlier, cinchona bark provides quinine, which is still a primary treatment for malaria. The opium poppy's most biologically active constituent, morphine, remains the standard against which new synthetic pain relievers are evaluated.

When plants are used to produce drugs, only those components that pharmacologists can identify as active (given the current state of their science, which is certainly far advanced from a hundred years ago, but hopefully less advanced than it will be a hundred years from now) are used. These components are extracted from the plant's balanced, synergistically intertwined matrix of minerals, vitamins, bioflavonoids, glycosides, alkaloids, and numerous other substances known and unknown whose role we do not yet understand. The extracted components are then chemically altered in some way—because if a drug is not a substance never before seen in nature, the pharmaceutical company cannot patent it—and concentrated, so their effect is magnified many times.

The resulting drug is neither gentle in its action nor balanced. Drugs either block some normal physiological response (antihistamines, for example, prevent the mucus secretion the body uses to trap and flush away viruses and other pathogens) or take over some physiological function, supplanting normal activity with abnormal activity (for example, diuretics, prescribed for congestive heart failure, cause the body to eliminate fluid along with potassium, magnesium, and every other mineral, which can cause serious problems, including irregular heart rhythms). In contrast, herbal medicines are natural in origin. Their physiological actions are gentle and balanced. They do not disrupt; rather, they support the body's regulatory and defense systems. In doing so, herbal medicines strengthen the body so it can eliminate the cause of the problem.

Drugs not only do not eliminate the causes of the vast majority of health problems—your child does not develop an ear infection because she is antibiotic deficient—but they frequently cause side effects, some of them deadly. A study published April 15, 1998, in the *Journal of the American Medical Association,* reported that in 1994, 2,216,000 hospitalized patients in the United States suffered adverse drug reactions (ADRs), and 106,000 of them died. These ADRs were not the result of inappropriately used drugs; the drugs were properly prescribed and taken in the prescribed amounts.

Where children are concerned, these statistics are reason for extreme caution with regard to drugs. Children's immature organ systems do not process drugs as if they were miniaturized adults, and most conventional drugs are not tested on children before gaining FDA approval. A 1990 study by the U.S. Government's General Accounting Office reviewed 198 new drugs approved by the FDA between 1976 and 1985. More than half of these drugs caused serious side effects that were not detected until several years after the drugs had been in widespread use. The same report found that drugs reviewed by the FDA for use in children were twice as likely to lead to serious reactions as those approved for use by adults. Severe reactions included heart failure, anaphylactic shock, convulsions, kidney and liver failure, severe blood disorders, blindness, and death.

Drugs do have their place. They are definitely appropriate in a crisis where normal physiological responses, such as inflammation or fever, have become so excessive that they become part of the problem, or where a virulent bug is winning over the immune system's defenses. In such instances, the suppressive effects of drugs can save your child's life. After the crisis, consider alternatives. The following herbal medicines will help you enable your child to develop the kind of truly resilient immune system that will keep her healthy and vital. They are the herbal remedies you will rely on as essential components of your natural home pharmacy.

Types of Herbal Preparations

Herbal medicines are available both singly and in combinations, for internal use as tinctures, extracts, capsules and tablets, lozenges, and teas, and for external use as ointments, lotions, salves, and sprays.

Tinctures are liquid herbal preparations in which alcohol is used to extract the herb's medicinal constituents. Although concentrated and therefore potent, easy to administer (a dose ranges from 3 drops for an infant to 20 to 40 drops for a child over twelve), and well assimilated by the body, tinctures have their drawbacks. They are typically bitter or unpleasant tasting and contain alcohol, although even a 20-drop dose would provide only minute amounts. If even a minute amount of alcohol is of concern, simply add the dose of tincture to ¼ cup very hot water, let it sit for five minutes, and the alcohol will evaporate.

Extracts can be made using either alcohol or water; just check the label to see which extraction method was used. Otherwise, they are equivalent to tinctures.

Capsules and tablets contain ground-up or powdered raw herb. If these herbal pills do not contain a *standardized extract,* they will be much less potent than tinctures or extracts. Typically, a dose will consist of several pills, several times a day. If your child is able to swallow pills, you will avoid the unpleasant-taste issue. If not, you can open capsules or mash tablets, and add the dose to a small amount of fruit juice, applesauce, oatmeal, yogurt—any food your child likes.

Medicinal herbal teas can be found in numerous formulations targeting various ailments. Most taste delicious and provide a health-promoting way to give lots of fluids. Teas, however, are much less potent than tinctures, extracts, or pills.

Nursing mothers can sidestep even the minor difficulties associated with each of the internal herbal preparations by simply taking an adult dose of the necessary herbal medicine—its healing effect will be transmitted to the infant through the breast milk.

Ointments, lotions, salves, and sprays are applied topically to help heal broken skin and wounds (calendula for surface cuts and bruises; hypericin for deeper wounds), fight skin infections and rashes (goldenseal, echinacea), and heal skin irritations, minor burns, and sunburns (aloe vera, comfrey).

Age-Appropriate Dosages

Use the dosages below unless otherwise indicated in the description of specific herbal medicines that follows. Remember, each child grows and develops at different rates. If your child is two, six, or twelve, use the lower dosage level if she falls within the lower end of the normal range in height and weight for her age; use the higher dosage level if she falls within the upper end of the normal range in height and weight for her age.

Infant to Two Years. For one dose, use 3 drops extract or tincture diluted in ¼ cup water, breast milk, or 2 or 3 teaspoons of tea. As explained above, a nursing mother may simply take an adult dose, and the herb will be transmitted to her baby in her breast milk.

Two to Six Years. For one dose, use 6 to 10 drops extract or tincture diluted in ¼ cup water or ¼ cup tea, or mash ½ tablet or capsule and blend into a soft food your child likes.

Six to Twelve Years. For one dose, use 10 to 20 drops of extract or tincture, ½ cup of tea, or 1 tablet or capsule.

Twelve Years or Older. For one dose, use 20 to 40 drops extract or tincture, 1 cup of tea, or 2 tablets or capsules.

A Child's Basic Herbal Medicines

ALOE VERA GEL

A soothing remedy for all those childhood cuts, scrapes, scratches, and sunburns, aloe vera has long been valued for its anti-inflammatory, moisturizing, emollient, and antimicrobial properties. Applied topically, aloe vera gel enhances the healing of surface wounds (scrapes, cuts, and bruises), burns, and sunburns, and also will relieve the discomfort and promote healing of skin rashes, insect stings, and insect bites. Leave a bottle of aloe vera gel in your refrigerator for extra cooling relief.

BROMELAIN (capsules)

Obtained from the stem of the pineapple plant, bromelain's primary claim to fame is its use in reducing the pain, inflammation, and edema associated with sports-related injuries, and significantly lessening healing time. Studies also have found that bromelain is effective in reducing the swelling, bruising, pain, and healing time associated with dental surgery, particularly when used both before and after surgery. Should your child need a tooth extraction, or should his braces need to be adjusted, bromelain may help. It should be taken on an empty stomach, one age-appropriate dose three times a day between meals.

CALENDULA (ointment, lotion, spray)

Commonly known as the marigold, calendula's orange and yellow flowers grace many gardens throughout Europe and North America. Rich in flavonoids, saponins, and carotenoids, calendula is both anti-inflammatory and antiseptic. Gently apply calendula lotion or use calendula spray as you would Bactine to naturally lessen discomfort and speed healing of minor burns, sunburns, skin irritations, eczema, and rashes. Calendula spray is another good remedy to leave in the refrigerator for cooling relief.

CAROB (powder)

Finally, a remedy with a taste your child will love. Carob pods, ground into powder that greatly resembles cocoa in both appearance and taste, have been effectively used for centuries to treat diarrhea. Carob's main constituents are large sugar molecules and tannins. When added to liquid, carob's sugars become a gummy thickener that absorbs water and helps solidify loose stools. Carob's tannins bind to and inactivate toxins and inhibit the growth of bacteria—two actions that also help treat diarrhea.

CATNIP (extract, tincture, capsules, tea)

A gentle sedative, catnip is a child's valerian (a renowned herbal sedative for adults). Catnip's essential oil contains a sedative constituent that helps induce sleep and soothe coughs.

CHAMOMILE (flower extract, tincture, tea)

Chamomile flowers contain numerous biologically active constituents, including several bioflavonoids, notably quercetin. Chamomile has long been valued for its anti-inflammatory, antispasmodic, and smooth muscle-relaxing effects, especially in the gastrointestinal tract. Turn to chamomile when your child has an upset stomach or when muscular tension is preventing her from relaxing and falling asleep.

COMFREY (gel, ointment, tea)

Comfrey root contains a substance called allantoin, which promotes tissue growth and is healing to the skin. It is frequently an ingredient in ointments and salves for irritated or inflamed skin conditions such as burns, sunburn, eczema, and scabies. If you don't have a comfrey ointment, you can soak a clean white cloth in cooled comfrey tea and apply the compress to the skin.

ECHINACEA AND GOLDENSEAL COMBINATION (root tincture)

Working in tandem, enchinacea and goldenseal boost immune defenses against both viruses and bacteria. This is the herbal remedy to turn to when your child comes down with a cold, flu, or ear infection. During the first 72 hours of its use, echinacea significantly increases the production of interferon—an important part of the body's defense against viral infections such as colds and flu. In addition, echinacea boosts the activity of other immune cells (white blood cells, lymphocytes, and macrophages) that defend against bacteria as well as viruses. Goldenseal is an herbal antibiotic effective against a wide spectrum of infection-causing bacteria. The immune boost these herbs provide is immediate and dramatic—they are not meant to be used constantly but to be taken when needed. Neither the combination formula nor either herb should be taken regularly; use only as needed and then for no more than one week at a time. If necessary, alternate one week on, one week off.

GARLIC (deodorized capsules or fresh cloves)

An antibiotic, antiseptic, antifungal, and antihelmintic (antiparasite and worm), garlic can help cleanse and protect the intestinal tract from undesirable critters, including *Candida albicans* (yeast infections). Garlic also supports cardiovascular health by lowering cholesterol and triglyceride levels, inhibiting platelet stickiness, and increasing fibrinolysis. Through these combined actions, garlic helps keep blood thin so it flows well and doesn't clump up. If your child gets frequent stomach upsets or is often flatulent, fresh garlic may help. If cardiovascular disease runs in your family, you and your child will benefit from garlic. And no one else has to suffer—deodorized garlic tablets and capsules are small enough to be easily swallowed by most children.

GINGER (root extract, tincture, capsules, tea, fresh root)

An all-around tonic for the digestive tract, ginger stimulates digestion, keeps intestinal muscles toned (which facilitates the transport of food through the digestive system), and alleviates nausea and vomiting. All this and it tastes delicious too! For the health of your child's digestive tract, add ginger to stir-fries, juice a sliver of ginger root with apples or carrots, or bake ginger cookies or gingery apple or pumpkin pie. If the thought of food is far from appealing, try ginger tea, tincture, or capsules. If your child has a tendency to get motion sickness, give one or two doses of ginger the day before the trip. Should your child become nauseated while traveling, a dose of ginger can be given every two to three hours.

GOLDENSEAL (root extract, tincture, capsules, tea)

Because of its antimicrobial activity, in addition to its use in combination with echinacea for colds, flu, and other respiratory infections, goldenseal has a long history of use for infectious diarrhea and vaginal infections. It also can be used topically as a poultice to heal boils and infected scrapes and cuts. To make a poultice, simply open a capsule or two, mix with enough water to make a paste, apply to the infected area, and cover with a bandage. Change the poultice twice daily.

LICORICE (root extract, tincture, tea)

Several biologically active constituents—glycyrrhizin, flavonoids, and antioxidants—give licorice its demulcent (soothing, coating), anti-inflammatory, and antiviral properties. Licorice is an excellent remedy for upset tummies and irritated urinary tracts. Most children love the taste; the tea is naturally sweet, so it's especially useful when your child has a cold, cough, or sore throat—times when his immune system does *not* need a spoonful of sugar! (Just 3 ounces of sugar—the amount in a couple of glasses of juice—typically causes at least a 40 percent reduction in neutrophil activity that starts less than thirty minutes after ingestion and lasts over five hours. Neutrophils constitute 60 to 70 percent of circulating white blood cells, so shutting them down can seriously impair the immune system.)

PEPPERMINT (leaf extract, tincture, tea, capsule)

Peppermint is a carminative that eases intestinal cramping and tones the digestive system. It can be used to aid digestion and relieve nausea, diarrhea, gas, and heartburn. Since peppermint contains menthol, it is also cooling and can help reduce fever. If you also are giving your child a homeopathic remedy, however, don't use peppermint for at least a half-hour before and a half-hour after you give the homeopathic medicine, as the menthol in peppermint may antidote the remedy.

PSYLLIUM SEED

Psyllium seed is a gentle, bulk-forming laxative high in both fiber and mucilage. When the husk of the seed comes into contact with water, it swells and forms a gelatinous mass that keeps the stool hydrated and soft. The increased bulk stimulates the bowel walls to contract and eliminate their contents—and your child's constipation.

SLIPPERY ELM (loose bark, lozenges)
Its mucilage gives slippery elm the soothing, lubricating effects for which it is named. Taken internally, slippery elm can help heal an inflamed throat or intestinal tract. Slippery elm lozenges taste pleasant and will soothe your child's sore throat. Slippery elm tea will settle the intestines, helping to normalize either diarrhea or constipation due to dry, hard stools. To make tea, mix powdered slippery elm bark with heated water, steep a couple of minutes, and drink.

MEDICINAL FOODS AND VITAMIN AND MINERAL SUPPLEMENTS

The following supplements provide key nutrients for an optimally functioning immune system and should become regular additions to your child's diet—with the exception of those in the "Use as needed" category.

Use as Needed

ACTIVATED CHARCOAL CAPSULES
Activated charcoal—not ground-up briquets, but medicinal charcoal—helps absorb poisons and gas. Within fifteen to twenty minutes, your child's gas, bloating, and flatulence will be significantly lessened, if not altogether gone. Her next bowel movement will be much darker than usual, as it will be colored by the charcoal. If your child is too small to swallow the capsules, just open them and stir the powder into a small glass of water. Room-temperature water is best; cold water may exacerbate symptoms.

PROBIOTICS
Not all bacteria are harmful. Some, called probiotics, are downright essential for proper functioning of our digestive tracts. In their normal life cycle, these friendly bacteria produce B vitamins and enzymes that help us digest our food; they also crowd out unfriendly bacteria that can infect the intestines, urinary tract, and vagina. The most potent healing probiotic strains are *L. acidophilus* (which produces its own natural antibiotics), *B. bifidum* (which crowds out unhealthy yeast and bacteria and assists the liver), and *L. rhamno-*

sus (which defends against food allergies). Should your child be given a course of antibiotics for an ear infection, these drugs will kill not only the bad bacteria that cause the infection but also the good bacteria in your child's intestines. If any harmful bacteria have survived after these healthy strains are killed off, they are free to multiply unchecked, and your child's intestines are left wide open and vulnerable to whatever bacteria arrive first. Think about all the things your child's hands touch, then think about how often her hands touch her face, eyes, nose, and ears. Make sure a significant number of probiotics are on hand to protect her intestines. If your child has not been given antibiotics but frequently has bad breath or digestive problems such as bloating, gas, or diarrhea, this may signify that her intestinal ecology is out of balance. Give her supplemental probiotics.

Look for probiotics in the refrigerator case at your health food store or natural foods grocery. Be sure to check the expiration date. The glass jars in which they are sold will contain either capsules or powder. Follow dosage directions on the bottle. Probiotics should be taken on an empty stomach with a glass of room-temperature water—first thing in the morning works best.

FOS

A naturally occurring substance in fruit and vegetables, FOS, short for *fructooligosaccharides,* is the favorite food of probiotics. FOS looks like finely granulated white sugar and tastes quite sweet. If you're giving your child probiotics, it helps to keep these friendly bacteria healthy and well nourished, as they colonize your child's intestines. Sprinkle a spoonful over your child's morning cereal or mix it into his morning drink.

QUERCETIN

Quercetin is a member of a group of compounds that impart the blue and red colors in plants. Called bioflavonoids or flavonoids, these compounds are much more than plant pigments. Among the more than 4,000 flavonoids that have now been identified, most are antioxidants. The bioflavonoid proanthocyanidin, found in red grape juice and red wine, is thought to strengthen capillary walls and protect against heart disease. The flavonoids in green tea, called catechins, not only protect the heart but are thought to prevent cancer. Of all the bioflavonoids discovered to date, quercetin is the one with the highest antiallergy activity. Quercetin stops allergies via its anti-inflammatory and antihistamine actions. It prevents nasal passages, lungs, and eyes from swelling on contact with an allergen and prevents the release of those itchy chemicals that make the nose run and the eyes water. Unlike drugs, quercetin does not cause cottony mouths, noses and throats so dry they become sore, or drowsiness. Unlike NSAIDs (non-steroidal anti-inflammatory drugs, such as Advil and Motrin), which are currently the leading cause of gastric bleeding in the United States, quercetin has been shown to protect the gastric mucosa from damage even after NSAIDs were taken.

ZINC LOZENGES

Zinc is a critical nutrient for healthy immune function and, like vitamin C, possesses direct antiviral activity. Several double-blind, placebo-controlled studies have now demonstrated that zinc lozenges can lessen symptoms and shorten the duration of the common cold. However, only certain lozenge formulations were effective. These were the lozenges that used the amino acid glycine as a sweetener and did not contain citric acid, mannitol, or sorbitol as sweetening agents. For the zinc to be effective, it must be ionized in saliva. Glycine does not prevent the ionization of zinc in saliva, whereas citric acid, mannitol, and sorbitol do. If your child feels a cold or sore throat coming on, give her zinc glycine lozenges supplying 15 milligrams of elemental zinc to dissolve in her mouth every two waking hours after an initial double dose. Use zinc lozenges for up to seven days.

What to Add to Your Child's Diet

EMERGEN-C

An Alacer Corporation nutritional product that comes in packets, Emergen-C is a good daily supplement and an absolute lifesaver on trips or during an acute illness. Each packet makes a fizzy drink containing 1,000 milligrams of vitamin C, plus B vitamins, calcium, magnesium, potassium, sodium, manganese, chromium, and zinc. It comes in various kid-friendly flavors, so chances are your child will like at least one. Even if you don't use it daily, keep several packets in your purse. When your child starts sneezing on the airplane, or after his next soccer game, when he is hot, thirsty, dripping with sweat (which may mean he is depleted of various minerals), and suddenly feels chilly, reach for the Emergen-C.

FLAXSEED OIL

Your child needs essential fatty acids (EFAs) to maintain her health—especially the health of her immune system—and her body cannot manufacture them. Instead, she must get them from the foods she eats or from supplements. According to Leo Galland, M.D., author of *Super Immunity for Kids,* many researchers and clinicians believe our health, and that of our children, is at risk because we are seriously deficient in EFAs for a combination of reasons. EFAs are found in certain nuts, seeds, fish, and the oils derived from these foods—none of which are important staples in the diets of most Americans. EFAs are fragile and easily damaged by air, high temperatures, and food processing, so virtually none remains in most processed oils. Other types of fats, abundant in foods most Americans do consume regularly, fill up the biochemical spaces EFAs should inhabit. If we lack adequate amounts of other vitamins and minerals, we may not be able to use the EFAs we do manage to consume.

EFAs are a vital component of all the body's membranes—from the membrane around each cell that allows it to function properly, to the mucous membranes that line the respiratory and digestive tracts, to the skin, the body's outermost membrane. Symptoms indicating inadequate EFAs include dry, scaly, rough, or bumpy skin; rashes and acne; brittle nails; hair that is flat and dull; and recurrent infections. EFA deficiency can be a significant contributing factor to irritable bowels, allergies, asthma, PMS, menstrual cramps, and juvenile rheumatoid arthritis.

Flaxseed oil is an excellent vegetarian source of essential fatty acids—but only if it is organic, cold pressed, refrigerated, and packaged in a dark, opaque bottle (remember, EFAs are fragile and must be handled with care). Be sure to check the expiration date. Freshly pressed, organic flaxseed oil has a delicious, slightly sweet but very mild taste. If the oil tastes the least bit bitter, throw it out—it's rancid. Give your child 1 tablespoon of flaxseed oil each day. Don't use it for frying or sautéing—high heat and oxygen destroy EFAs. Instead, mix flaxseed oil into oatmeal (after cooking, not before), use it with lemon juice or vinegar as a salad dressing, drizzle it over baked or steamed vegetables, or dip pieces of bread in it as you would with olive oil. Kept refrigerated, flaxseed oil should remain fresh for four to six weeks.

FLAXSEED MEAL

If your child has trouble with constipation, or if you just want to add more fiber to his diet, flaxseed meal is a great way to do so, since it also will provide essential fatty acids. Freshly ground organic flaxseed meal has a sweet, nutty taste. Sprinkle it over salads, mix it into dips, or add a spoonful to a bowl of soup, cold cereal, or cooked oatmeal. Encourage your teenager to make flaxseed a daily habit. Flaxseed meal is the best internal cosmetic for beautiful skin. It can help turn blotchy, pimply skin into a clear, radiant complexion. Purchase organic flaxseed and grind as needed in a coffee grinder or blender, or buy already-ground organic flaxseed meal—it should be in the refrigerator case near the flaxseed oil at your health food store or wholefoods grocery. Check the expiration date. Stored in the refrigerator, flaxseed meal should remain fresh for four to six weeks; stored in the freezer, it should last eight to ten weeks.

FISH OIL EXTRACTS

If your child's skin problems do not resolve using flaxseed oil, try fish-oil extract capsules. Marketed under brand names such as Max EPA, these essential fatty acids from cold-water fatty fish (preferably salmon) have a slightly different mix of EFAs and are often effective in treating diseases associated with EFA deficiency. One caveat: your child must be able to swallow this oil in capsules; it has a very unpalatable taste.

CALCIUM AND MAGNESIUM COMBINATION FORMULA

Calcium and magnesium relax muscles, improve blood flow, soothe a keyed-up or stressed nervous system, and often decrease a child's craving for sugar. Calcium is essential for your child's growing bones and truly becomes critical should he suffer a bone fracture. In addition, a combination calcium and magnesium supplement will help your child relax and heal in any condition in which tense or aching muscles, stress, or nervousness is a factor. All the following conditions signal a need for additional calcium and magnesium: bedwetting, headache, hyperactivity, influenza, insomnia, mononucleosis, muscle or menstrual cramps, or seizures. One dose of liquid combination formula contains 250 milligrams of calcium and 125 milligrams of magnesium.

VITAMIN E

Vitamin E is a very important antioxidant for the heart, blood lipids, and cell membranes. Pollution, sun exposure, heavy exercise, the polyunsaturated fats found in refined vegetable oils—all increase free-radical production and our need for vitamin E. In studies in which athletes were given vitamin E before strenuous exercise, they suffered less free-radical damage and less muscle soreness, and recovered faster. Applied topically, vitamin E will reduce the redness, inflammation, and skin sensitivity associated with sunburn. The RDA for vitamin E is not met by the typical American diet. The best food sources of vitamin E—unrefined vegetable oils, wheat germ, liver, and eggs—are high-fat foods, making it difficult to healthfully consume protective levels of this nutrient without using supplements. Your child will love Nature's Plus carob-flavored chewable vitamin E capsules, and one given with breakfast will lessen oxidative damage from sun exposure on the ski slopes, or during those long summer days playing at the park, beach, or in your backyard. If your child should get a sunburn, prick open a capsule of vitamin E and apply gently for immediate relief and to speed healing.

PROTEIN POWDER

Just a tablespoon of protein powder a day—rice or soy-based for children sensitive or allergic to dairy—can help ensure picky eaters, especially if they are picky vegetarians, get adequate, high-quality protein. Add a spoonful to oatmeal, home-baked muffins, smoothies, juice, or milk.

BREWER'S YEAST

A nutritional, food-grade yeast, Brewer's is a wonderful source of B vitamins and trace minerals. Its peanutty flavor makes it a welcome addition to oatmeal, soups, and homemade muffins and cookies—or sprinkle a spoonful over lightly buttered popcorn.

BLACKSTRAP MOLASSES

Organic, unsulphured blackstrap molasses is a good source of iron, especially for vegetarian children. Use blackstrap sparingly, though, because its distinctive flavor will overpower. Blackstrap tastes great in gingerbread, ginger cookies, and baked beans.

Appendix B

A Parent's Natural Home Health Kit*

BASIC MEDICAL SUPPLIES

- Ace bandage (don't forget the clips to secure it)
- Bandages (in a variety of sizes—small to large, round, and rectangular)
- Gauze pads (100 percent sterile cotton)
- Clear surgical adhesive tape
- Cotton balls (100 percent sterile cotton)
- Disinfectant—Aromatherapy Disinfectant Blend: In a small glass dropper bottle, mix 10 drops lavender, 10 drops eucalyptus, and 20 drops thyme. Use 10 drops of the blend in a pint of warm water in a bowl for washing. A drop of lavender or tea tree oil also can be applied directly to the bandage used to cover an abrasion. Or, in a small glass dropper bottle, combine 15 drops tea tree oil with 2 tablespoons cold-pressed, organic vegetable oil and store in refrigerator. After washing with warm water and mild soap, apply a couple of drops of this mixture directly to the abrasion and cover with a bandage.
- Mist humidifier
- Eye dropper (use to administer liquid medicines to infants)
- Nasal bulb syringe (use for infants and toddlers who need help clearing their sinuses)

---

*By contributing author Lara Pizzorno, M.A. (Div.), M.A. (Lit.), L.M.T.

- Lip balm (look for petroleum-free products based on soothing, healing, safe beeswax)

- Sunscreen (look for sunscreen that is aluminum and PABA-free)

- Baby powder (look for powder that is aluminum and talcum free, such as powder made from cornstarch)

- Hot-water bottle or moist heat electric-heating pad

- Ice pack (gel-filled, preferably in a case with Velcro closures, so it can be wrapped around a waist, knee, arm, or shoulder; leave in the freezer so it's ready when needed)

- Calamine lotion (for inflammatory skin conditions, e.g., poison ivy, chickenpox, heat rash)

- Epsom salts (add to baths for sore, aching, or strained muscles)

- Aveeno or organic rolled oats and cheesecloth (follow directions on the container, and add to warm bath for itching, sunburn, and skin irritations including rashes, measles, chickenpox, eczema, impetigo, hives)

- Antibacterial liquid soap or spray (usually based on tea tree oil and/or lavender; keep purse-size waterless and spray versions in your car's glove compartment and your child's lunchbox or backpack)

- Socks (Cotton socks plus a pair of heavy wool socks big enough to be worn over the cotton ones. To lower high fevers quickly and safely: soak the cotton socks in cold water, wring them out, and put them on your child's feet. Immediately put the wool socks over the wet cotton ones. Put your child back under the bedcovers. Within fifteen to thirty minutes, the cotton socks will be dry, and the fever should have dropped.)

- Sterilized needle (use to remove splinters, then re-sterilize before putting away)

- Scissors with rounded tips (use to safely remove bandages; great for home haircuts, too)

- Sling and safety pins (or large bandanna to use as an emergency sling)

- Tweezers (Slightly rounded edges are easier. Use to remove wood or glass splinters once they are near the surface.)
- Thermometer (Avoid glass. Single-use stick-on tape thermometers are available for infants; metal and plastic digital-readout thermometers for use under the arm or tongue are quick and safe for toddlers and older children.)

AROMATHERAPY ESSENTIAL OILS

- Chamomile
- Clove
- Dill
- Eucalyptus
- Geranium
- Lavender
- Lemon
- Peppermint
- Rosemary
- Tea tree
- Thyme linalol (a species usually grown at high altitudes, thyme linalol is slightly more expensive, but its chemical composition is particularly effective for children)
- Glycerin (useful as a medium in which to dissolve essential oils used for mouthwashes, etc.)
- Cold-pressed vegetable oil (used as a medium for aromatherapy oils)
- Beeswax (used with essential oils in salve to eliminate head lice)
- Castor oil (used with essential oils in salve to eliminate head lice)
- Rock salt (used with essential oils in foot baths)
- Green clay or aluminum-free talc (used in preparation of medicinal foot powders)

HOMEOPATHIC MEDICINES

- Aconitum
- *Allium cepa*
- *Anas barbariae* (marketed under the name *Oscillococcinum*)
- *Apis mellifica*
- *Arnica montana*
- *Arsenicum album*
- Belladonna
- *Bryonia alba*
- *Calcarea carbonica*
- Cantharis
- Chamomilla
- Euphrasia
- Gelsemium
- Hypericum
- Ignatia
- *Kali bichromicum*
- *Ledum palustre*
- *Magnesia phosphorica*
- Mercurius
- *Nux vomica*
- Pulsatilla
- *Rhus toxicodendron*
- *Ruta graveolens*
- Sulphur

Homeopathic Combination Medicines

- Similisan (homeopathic eyedrops)
- Traumeel (arnica ointment)

HERBAL MEDICINES

- Aloe vera gel
- Calendula cream
- Calendula spray (replaces Bactine)
- Catnip alcohol-free extract and/or tea
- Chamomile alcohol-free extract and/or tea
- Comfrey gel
- Cough and bronchial syrup (Boericke & Tafel Sugar-free)
- Echinacea and goldenseal combination tincture
- Goldenseal root capsules
- Garlic, in deodorized capsules or fresh
- Ginger alcohol-free extract, tea, and/or fresh root
- Licorice root alcohol-free extract and/or tea
- Slippery elm lozenges

Herbal Combination Formulas

- KID B-Well Tonic (Nature's Answer immune tonic containing alcohol-free organic extracts of astragalus, burdock, and dandelion)
- Nat-Choo (Nature's Answer children's cold and flu formula containing alcohol-free organic extracts of echinacea, catnip, peppermint, boneset, and eyebright)
- Super Immuno-Comp (Enzymatic Therapy immune-stimulating formula, capsules containing astragalus, echinacea, goldenseal, shiitake mushroom, and licorice root)
- Tummie Tonic (Nature's Answer blend of alcohol-free organic extracts of meadowsweet, chamomile, angelica, slippery elm, ginger, and fennel to soothe and relieve upset stomach)

MEDICINAL SUPPLEMENTS:
FOODS, VITAMINS, AND MINERALS

Use as Needed

- Activated charcoal capsules (helps relieve gas, bloating, flatulence)
- Probiotics (re-establishes healthy intestinal flora after a course of antibiotics)
- FOS (fructooligosaccharides; probiotics' favorite food)
- Quercetin (helps quench environmental allergies, sinusitis, hay fever)
- Zinc lozenges (helps lessen severity of symptoms and shorten duration of colds and sore throats)

Add to Your Child's Diet

- Emergen-C (Alacer Corporation product containing vitamin C, B vitamins, calcium, magnesium, potassium, sodium, manganese, chromium, and zinc)
- Flaxseed oil (a vegetarian source of essential fatty acids)
- Flaxseed meal (provides essential fatty acids and fiber)
- Fish oil extracts (essential fatty acids from cold-water fatty fish, preferably salmon)
- Calcium and magnesium combination formula (liquid for children too young to swallow a capsule or in capsule form)
- Vitamin E (chewable tablets or in capsules)
- Protein powder (rice or soy-based for children sensitive or allergic to dairy)
- Brewer's yeast (nutritional, food-grade yeast, source of B vitamins and trace minerals)
- Blackstrap molasses (organic, unsulphured—a good source of iron)

Bibliography

Bernstein, J., S. Alpert, K. Nauss, and R. Suskind. "Depression of Lymphocyte Transformation Following Oral Glucose Ingestion." *American Journal of Clinical Nutrition* 30 (1977): 613.

Cockburn, F., et al. "Effect of Diet on the Fatty Acid Composition of the Major Phospholipids of Infant Cerebral Cortex." *Archives of Disease in Childhood* 72, no. 3 (March 1995): 198–203.

Coulter, Harris, Ph.D. *Vaccination, Social Violence, and Criminality: The Medical Assault on the American Brain.* Berkeley, Calif.: North Atlantic Books, 1990.

Coulter, Harris, Ph.D., and Barbara Fisher. *DPT: A Shot in the Dark.* Garden City, N.Y.: Avery, 1991.

Dennison, B.A. "Fruit Juice Consumption by Infants and Children: A Review." *Journal of the American College of Nutrition* 17 (1998): 371–78.

de Shazo, R.D., and S.F. Kemp. "Allergic Reactions to Drugs and Biologic Agents." *Journal of the American Medical Association* 278, no. 22 (December 10, 1977): 1895–906.

Dewey, Kathryn. "Differences in Morbidity Between Breast-fed and Formula-Fed Infants." *Journal of Pediatrics* 126 (1995): 696–702.

Duke, James, Ph.D. *The Green Pharmacy.* Emmaus, Penn.: Rodale Press, 1997.

Eisenberg, Arlene, Heidi E. Murkoff, and Sandee Eisenberg Hathaway. *What to Expect the First Year.* New York: Workman Publishing, 1996.

Eisenberg, D.M., et al. "Unconventional Medicine in the United States— Prevalence, Costs, and Patterns of Use." *New England Journal of Medicine* 328, no. 4 (January 28, 1993): 246–52.

Farquharson, J., et al. "Effect of Diet on Infant Subcutaneous Tissue Triglyceride Fatty Acids." *Archives of Disease in Childhood* 69 (1993): 589–93.

Fulder, Stephen, and John Blackwood. *Garlic: Nature's Original Remedy*. Berkeley, Calif.: Healing Arts Press, 1991.

Galland, Leo, M.D. *Super Immunity for Kids*. New York: Dell Publishing, 1988.

Gordon, Jay. *Good Food Today, Great Kids Tomorrow*. Los Angeles: Michael Wiese Productions, 1994.

Hoffman, D.R., et al "Effects of Supplementation with Omega-3 Long-chain Polyunsaturated Fatty Acids on Retinal and Cortical Development in Premature Infants." *American Journal of Clinical Nutrition* 57 (1993): 807S–812S.

Kramer, F.M., et al. "Breast-feeding Reduces Maternal Lower-Body Fat." *Journal of the American Dietetic Association* 93, no. 4 (April 1993): 429–33.

La Leche League. *The Womanly Art of Breast-feeding*. Franklin Park, Ill.: La Leche League International Publishing, 1992.

Lazarou, J., B.H. Pomeranz, and P.N. Corey. "Incidence of Adverse Drug Reactions in Hospitalized Patients: A Meta-analysis of Prospective Studies." *Journal of the American Medical Association* 279, no. 15 (April 15, 1998): 1200–5.

Lucas, A. "Randomised Trial of Early Diet in Preterm Babies and Later Intelligence Quotient." *British Medical Journal* 317, no. 1717 (November 1998): 1481–87.

Makrides, M., et al. "Are Long-chain Polyunsaturated Fatty Acids Essential Nutrients in Infancy?" *The Lancet* (June 10, 1995) 345: 1463–68.

Mars, Brigitte. *Elder*. Los Angeles: Keats Publishing, 1997.

Mazzarella, Barbara. *Bach Flower Remedies for Children*. Rochester, Vt.: Healing Arts Press, 1994.

Merck Manual of Medical Information. Whitehouse Station, N.J.: Merck Research Laboratories, 1997.

Mindell, Earl, Ph.D. *Parents' Nutrition Bible*. Carson, Calif.: Hay House Publishing, 1992.

Mowrey, Daniel B. *The Scientific Validation of Herbal Medicine.* Los Angeles: Keats Publishing, 1994.

Murray, Michael, N.D. *Encyclopedia of Nutritional Supplements.* Rocklin, Calif.: Prima Publishing, 1996.

Murray, Michael. *The Healing Power of Herbs.* Rocklin, Calif.: Prima Publishing, 1995.

Murray, Michael, N.D., and Joseph Pizzorno, N.D. *The Encyclopedia of Natural Medicine, 2d ed.* Rocklin, Calif.: Prima Publishing, 1998.

Santillo, Humbart, N.D., Subhuti Dharmananda, and Robert S. Mendelsohn. *Natural Healing with Herbs.* Prescott, Ariz.: Hohm Press, 1984.

Schmidt, K. "Antioxidant Vitamins and Beta-Carotene: Effects on Immuno-competence." *American Journal of Clinical Nutrition* 53 (1991): 383S–385S.

Solter, Aletha, Ph.D. *The Aware Baby.* Goleta, Calif.: Shining Star Press, 1989.

Spock, Benjamin, M.D. *Baby and Child Care, 7th ed.* New York: Pocket Books, 1998.

Ullman, Dana, M.P.H. *Homeopathic Medicine for Children and Infants.* New York: G.P. Putnam's Sons, 1992.

Ullman, Dana, and Stephen Cummings. *Everybody's Guide to Homeopathic Medicines, 3d. ed.* Los Angeles: J.P. Tarcher, 1997.

Wenner, Paul. *Garden Cuisine.* New York: Simon & Schuster, 1997.

Winter, Ruth. *A Consumer's Dictionary of Cosmetic Ingredients, 4th ed.* New York: Crown, 1994.

Worwood, Valerie Ann. *The Complete Book of Essential Oils and Aromatherapy.* San Rafael, Calif.: New World Library, 1991.

Zand, Janet, L.Ac., O.M.D., Rachel Walton, R.N., and Bob Rountree, M.D. *Smart Medicine for a Healthier Child.* Garden City Park, N.Y.: Avery, 1994.

Index

('b' indicates boxed material)

A

Acellular DPT (DTaP) vaccine, 22, 26–27
Aches and pains, treatments for, 70
Acne and pimples, treatments for, 71–72
Aconitum (aconite), 167–168
Acupressure, 137
Addictions, and control patterns, 33
Adolescents, homocysteine levels in, 148
Alar, 18
Alcohol, while breast-feeding, 4
Allergies
  and breast milk, 7, 63
  to herbal medicine, 121
  treatments for, 72–77
  and vaccines, 23
Allium cepa (red onion), 168
Aloe vera gel, 71, 102, 184, 199
American ginseng (*Panax quinque-folinus*)
  endangered, 124
  and immune function, 52
Anas barbariae (heart and liver of duck), 168
Antibacterial components, of breast milk, 5
Antibiotics, and developing immune system, 50
Antibodies
  in breast milk, 4, 6, 50
  in colostrum, 7
Antiviral components, of breast milk, 5

Anxiety and restlessness, treatments for, 77–78
Apis mellifica (crushed bee), 168–169
Arnica montana, 169
Aromatherapy, 67, 154–161
  for aches and pains, 70
  for acne and pimples, 71
  for anxiety and restlessness, 77
  for asthma, 76
  for athlete's foot, 78
  for bedwetting, 99
  for boils, 79
  for burns, 80
  for chickenpox, 106
  for cold sores, 85
  for colic, 67
  for common cold, 84
  for conjunctivitis, 95
  for constipation, 102
  for coughs, 87
  for cuts, scrapes, and puncture wounds, 81
  for diaper rash, 68
  for diarrhea, 104
  for earache, 93–94
  for eczema, 72
  for fever, 89
  for fretfulness, 69
  for gas, indigestion, and nausea, 105
  for hay fever, 73
  for head lice, 97–98
  for influenza, 90
  for insect bites and stings, 82–83
  for insomnia, 100
  for laryngitis, 92

for measles, 108
for mumps, 110
for rubella, 109
for sinusitis, 74–75
for sore throat, 92
for styes, 96
for sunburn, 101
for teething, 69–70
for warts, 113
Aromatherapy Disinfectant Blend, 195
Aromatherapy essential oils, home health kit, 197
Arsenicum album (white arsenic), 169–170
Asthma, treatments for, 76–77
Athlete's foot, treatments for, 78–79
Attention deficit disorder (ADD), 126
  flower essence treatment, 134
  homeopathy for, 129
Attention deficit hyperactivity disorder (ADHD), 126, 127
  homeopathy for, 129
Aware Baby, The, 31

B

Bach, Edward, 132, 133
Bach Flower Remedies, 131, 133
Bach Flower Remedies for Children, 132
Bad Guys, food category, 13
Balsam of Peru, 98
Baptisia tinctoria, immune enhancer, 57
Basic medical supplies, home health kit, 195–197
B cell lymphocytes, 49, 50
Bedwetting, treatments for, 99

Beliefs, sharing with child, 38
Belladonna (deadly nightshade), 67, 170–171
Bertani, Elizabeth, on spiritual training, 40
Bin herbs, 120
Bioflavonoids, 189
Blackstrap molasses, 193, 200
Bland, Jeffrey, 16, 18
  on nutritional supplements, 143, 148
  on spiritual training, 38
Boil Bathing Solution, 79
Boils, treatments for, 79–80
Borage, added to formula, 9
Breast milk
  antibodies, in, 4, 6
  essential fatty acids in, 7
  nutrients, 4
Breast-feeding
  choosing, 4
  emotional advantages, 4–5
  mother's health during, 8
Brewer's yeast, 193, 200
British Medical Journal, on early nutrition, 145
British National Childhood Encephalopathy Study, 26
Bromelain, 184, 199
Bryonia alba (wild hops), 171
Buono, Nancy, 131, 132
Burns, treatments for, 80–81

C

Caffeine, while breast-feeding, 4
Calcarea carbonica (calcium carbonate), 171–172
Calcium and magnesium, 192, 200
Calendula, 68, 73, 185, 199
  for baby skin care, 62

Candida albicans, 17
Cantharus (Spanish fly), 172
Capsule, 120, 122, 183
Carbone, Michele, 23
Carob, 185
Cascara sagrada, dangers of, 121
Cassia, natural oil, 18
Catnip, 185
  tea, for fever, 58
Certified Herbologist (C.H.), 141
Chamomile (*chamomilla*), 69, 70, 76,
    78, 79, 82, 94, 101, 107, 108, 110,
    111, 156, 197, 172–173, 185, 199
Chamomile, German, 68, 72, 73, 74
Chamomile, Roman, 69, 77, 99, 100
Charcoal, activated, 188
Chi (vital life force), 134
Chickenpox (*varicella zoster*) vaccine,
    28–29
  treatments for, 106–107
Childhood viral infections, treatments
    for, 106–112
Children, treatments for common
    complaints, 70–112
Chinese medicine. *See* Oriental
    medicine
Chronic illness
  and Oriental medicine, 138
  and vaccinations, 21
Clove, 156, 197
Cold Sore Blend, 85
Cold sores, treatments for, 85–87
Colds, prevention recommendations,
    53b
Colic, treatments for, 67–68
Colostrum, 6, 7
Combination formulas, herbal, 199
Combinations, homeopathic
    medicines, 167, 199
Comfrey, 73, 83, 185, 199
Common cold, treatments for, 84–85

Conjunctivitis, treatments for, 95–96
Constipation, treatments for, 102–103
Consumers Union (CU), pesticide
    study, 13
*Consumer's Dictionary of Cosmetic
    Ingredients, A*, 61
Control patterns, pacifiers as, 33
Cool compresses, for fever, 58
Corn syrup, 18
Cortisol, reduced by crying, 34–35
Coughs, treatments for, 87–89
Coulter, Harris, 20, 23
Cow's milk, and allergic reactions, 8
Cradle cap, 62, 63–64
Crying
  encouraging in disturbed children,
    34
  importance of, 31
  responding to, 32
Cuts, scrapes, and puncture wounds,
    treatments for, 81–82

D

Dairy foods
  and mucus production, 51
  and psoriasis, 62
Dewey, Kathryn, 5
Diaper rash, 61, 62
  treatments for, 68–69
Diarrhea
  breast-fed versus formula-fed
    babies, 5, 6
  and fruit juice, 16
  treatments for, 103–104
Dietary habits, forming, 14
Digestive health, and fruit juice, 16
Dill, 157, 197
Diptheria vaccine, 25
"Discharge," negative feelings, 32

Disease mutation, and vaccine
  failure, 22
Docosahexaenoic acid (DHA), 7,
  145, 146
Dorfmeister, Heidi, on spiritual
  training, 41
DPT (diptheria–pertussis–tetanus)
  vaccine, 20, 22, 26–27
DPT: A Shot in the Dark, 20, 23
Duke, James, 115
  interview with, 117–122

E

Ear infections, 64–66
  breast-fed vs. formula-fed babies,
    5–6
  and cow's milk, 51
  remedies, 66b
Earache, treatments for, 93–95
Echinacea. *See also* Esberitox
  and Goldenseal, 75, 80, 86, 90, 91,
    93, 96, 98, 107, 109, 111, 186
  as immune enhancer, 51, 115
  and vitamin C prior to starting
    school, 50
E. coli, and meat, 14, 15
Eucalyptus, 73, 89, 157, 197
Eczema, 62, 63
  treatments for, 72–73
Elder flower syrup, for fever, 59
Emerald City Naturopathic Clinic,
  Seattle, Washington, 16
Emergen-C, 190, 200
Emotional nurturing, 31
Encyclopedia of Natural Medicine, 56
Endangered plants, 124
Energy fields, 133, 134
Environmental Protection Agency
  (EPA), on pesticides, 13

Ephedra, dangers of, 121
Ervolino, Frank, 58
Esberitox, 57, 60b, 117
Essential fatty acids (EFAs), 191, 192,
  200
  in breast milk, 7, 145
  function of, 145–146
Euphrasia (eyebright), 173
Extracts, 122, 183
Eye problems, treatments for, 95–97

F

Family Nurturing Center, Boulder,
  Colorado, 34
Ferrum phosphorus, 126
Fever
  allowed to run, 56, 57
  coping with, 60b
  danger signs, 59
  function of, 59
  homeopathic remedies for, 56
  treatments for, 89–90
Fish oil extracts, 192, 200
Fisher, Barbara, 20, 21, 24, 29
Flavonoids, 189
Flaxseed meal, 192, 200
Flaxseed oil, 191, 200
  added to formula, 9
Flexibility, with kids and health
  foods, 11–12
Flower essences
  description of, 132
  dosage, 136
  for children, 135b
Flu, prevention recommendations,
  53b
Food and Drug Administration
  (FDA), 20
Food Guide Pyramid for Children
  (USDA), 147

Food medicinal supplements, 188, 189
  home health kit, 200
Food-related Diarrhea Massage Oil formula, 104
Forms, herbal medicines, 120, 122, 182–183
FOS (fructooligosaccharides), 189
Fretfulness, treatments for, 69
Frey, William, 32
Fruit juice
  high sugar content, 16
  substitutes, 17, 18
Fungicide, garlic as, 78

G

Galland, Leo, 191
Garden Cuisine, 12
Garlic, 72, 74, 75, 76, 78, 117, 186
  antibiotic properties of, 52
Gas, indigestion and nausea, treatments for, 105–106
Gelsemium (yellow jasmine), 173
Generally Recognized As Safe (GRAS), 18
Geranium, 157, 197
German measles. *See* Rubella
Ginger, 105, 108, 116, 186–187
Goat's-milk-based formula, 8
Goldenseal, 76, 80, 82, 91, 104, 189
Good Food Today, Great Kids Tomorrow, 9
Good Guys, food category, 13
Gordon, Jay, 11
  on spiritual training, 44
Green Pharmacy, The, 115, 117, 120
Guillain-Barré syndrome
  and OPV, 26
  and tetanus vaccine, 27

H

Haemophilus influenza type B (Hib) vaccine, 27
Hahnemann, Samuel, 161, 162
Hamburgers, dangers of, 14, 15
Hand washing, 52
Hay fever, treatments for, 73–74
Head lice, treatments for, 96–97
Hepatitis B vaccine, 27–28
Herb products, first purchase tips, 119–120
Herb Research Foundation, Boulder, Colorado, 115
Herbal enema, for fever, 59
Herbal formulas, in Oriental medicine, 139, 140
Herbal medicines, 181–182
  dosage, 183–184
  for acne and pimples, 71–72
  for anxiety and restlessness, 78
  for asthma, 76
  for athlete's foot, 78
  for bedwetting, 99
  for boils, 80
  for burns, 81
  for chickenpox, 107
  for cold sores, 86
  for colic, 68
  for common cold, 85
  for conjunctivitis, 96
  for constipation, 103
  for coughs, 88
  for cuts, scrapes, and puncture wounds, 82
  for diaper rash, 68
  for diarrhea, 104
  for earache, 95
  for eczema, 73
  for fever, 90
  for fretfulness, 69

for gas, indigestion, and nausea, 105–106

for hay fever, 74

for head lice, 98

for influenza, 91

for insect bites and stings, 83

for insomnia, 101

for laryngitis, 93

for measles, 108

for mumps, 111

for rubella, 109–110

for sinusitis, 75

for sore throat, 93

for styes, 97

for sunburn, 102

for teething, 70

for warts, 113

home health kit, 199

types, 182–183

Herbal teas, for fever, 56

Herbs, selected by James Duke, 121, 123b

Herpes zoster (shingles), 29

Holding, 32, 35

Homeopathic Education Service, 164

Homeopathic Medicine for Children and Infants, 125

Homeopathic medicines/remedies, 166–167

  ear infection, 64

  fever, 60b

  home health kit, 198

Homeopathy, 125, 161–164

  for aches and pains, 71

  for acne and pimples, 71

  for anxiety and restlessness, 77–78

  for asthma, 76

  for athlete's foot, 78

  for bedwetting, 99

  for boils, 79

  for burns, 80–81

  for chickenpox, 106–107

  for cold sores, 86

  for colic, 67–68

  for common cold, 84–85

  for conjunctivitis, 96

  for constipation, 103

  for coughs, 87–88

  for cuts, scrapes, and puncture wounds, 82

  for diaper rash, 68

  for diarrhea, 104

  for earache, 94

  for eczema, 73

  for fever, 89–90

  for fretfulness, 69

  for gas, indigestion, and nausea, 105

  for hay fever, 73–74

  for head lice, 98

  for influenza, 90–91

  for insect bites and stings, 83

  for insomnia, 100–101

  for laryngitis, 92

  for measles, 108

  for mumps, 110–111

  for rubella, 109

  for sinusitis, 75

  for sore throat, 92

  for styes, 97

  for sunburn, 101

  for teething, 70

  for warts, 113

Homocysteine levels, in adolescents, 148

Hydrogenated oils

  in formula, 8

  and psoriasis, 62

Hyperactivity, definition, 127

Hypericum. *See* St. John's wort

Hyperkinesis. *See* Attention deficit hyperactivity disorder

I

Ignatia (St. Ignatius bean), 174
Immune system
  function of, 49–50
  impact of childhood vaccinations, 21
  in infants and young children, 50
Immunizations, risks of, 19, 21
Immunoglobins, 6, 7
Inactivated polio vaccine (IPV), 23
Inattention, defintion, 127
Individualization, in homeopathy, 162–163
Infantile scurvy, 150, 152
Infants
  treatments for common complaints, 67–70
  and vaccines, 29
  vitamin and mineral requirements, 145
Infection, and echinacea, 51
Influenza, treatments for, 90–91
Informed decision, vaccination, 30
Insect bites and stings, treatments for, 82–83
Insomnia, treatments for, 100–101
Interferon, and vitamin C, 50
International Association of Biological Standards, 24
International Foundation for Homeopathy, 164
Iron, 193
Itch Be Gone Lotion, 106

J

Joining in, 34
Journal of Pediatric Child Heath, 27
Journal of Pediatrics, 5

Journal of the American College of Nutrition, 16
Journal of the American Dietetic Association, 8
Journal of the American Medical Association, on pharmaceutical deaths, 115

K

Kali bichromicum (potassium bichromate), 175
Kava kava (*Piper methysticum*), relaxant properties of, 121, 123b
Kelly, Kim, 50
  prevention colds and flu, 53b

L

Lactobacillus acidophilus, 188
Lactobacillus bifidus, 7, 9
Lactose, in breast milk, 7
La Leche League, 3
Lancet, The
  on brain development in babies, 146
  on homeopathic medicines for asthma, 125
Laryngitis, treatments for, 92–93
Lavender, 71, 77, 79, 80, 81, 89, 90, 92, 99, 100, 157–158, 197
Law of similars, 125, 161
Laxmi (Faith Stone), on spiritual training, 41–44
Ledum palustre (wild rosemary, marsh tea), 175
Lemon, 71, 92, 158, 197
Licorice, 76, 189
"Like cures like," 125, 161

Linton, Molly, 16, 17
Listening relationship, 34
Lunch box foods, 15b
Lymphocytes, 49–50

M

Magnesia phosphorica (phospate of
    magnesium), 175–176
Mars, Brigitte, 62
    on spiritual training, 45
Materia medica
    for homeopathy, 163
    natural home pharmacy
        (Appendix A), 153–193
Manufacturer's reputation, 119
Mazzarella, Barbara, 132
McCaleb, Rob, 115
Measles, mumps, rubella (MMR)
    vaccine, 28
Measles treatments for, 108–109
Meat, chemicals in, 15
Meconium, 7
Medical exemption, vaccination, 30
Mercurius (mercury), 176
Meyer, Patricia, 132
Mindell, Earl, 13, 51
    on preventing colds and flu, 53b
Mineral deficiency, 118
Mineral supplements, 190, 192
    home health kit, 200
Minerals, 144–145
    RDAs for children, 152b
Mirroring feelings, 34
Modalities in homeopathy, 167
Monkey viruses, 23
Mullein oil, 95
Multiple vitamin-mineral supple-
    ments, purchasing, 143–144
Mumps treatments for, 110–112

Murray, Michael, 56, 57, 143, 145
    nutritional supplement recommen-
        dations, 149

N

National Center of Homeopathy, 164
National Commission for the
    Certification of Acupuncture
    and Oriental Medicine
    (NCCAOM), 141
National Institute of Health (NIH),
    on ADHD/ADD, 128
National Institute of Mental Health
    (NIMH), on ADHD/ADD, 127
National Vaccine Information Center,
    Vienna, VA, 19, 20
    questions to ask, 30
National Vaccine Injury Act (1986),
    20
Natrum muriaticum, 176–177
"Natural flavors," 18
Naturopathic doctors (NDs), 164
Negative emotions, and flower
    essences, 132
Nervous Agitation-related Diarrhea
    Massage Oil formula, 104
Non-steroidal anti-inflammatory
    drugs (NSAIDs), 190
North American Flower Essence
    Society, 133
Northwest Center for Homeopathic
    Medicine, Edmonds, Washington,
    126
Nursing, as control pattern, 33, 35
Nursing mothers, and herbal medi-
    cines, 183
Nutrients, in breast milk, 4, 145
Nutritional supplements, need for
    in children, 147, 148

Nux vomica (poison nut), 126, 166, 177–178, 198

O

Ointments, 183
Okay Guys, food category, 13
Omega-3 fatty acid, in breast milk, 7, 145, 146
Oral polio vaccine (OPV), 22, 25
Oriental medicine
  delivery system, 139
  features of, 138–139
  practitioner, choosing, 140–141
Oscillococcinum, 168
Osha root, 88
Otitis media, 64. *See also* Ear infections

P

Parents' Nutrition Bible, 13, 51
Peppermint, 105, 116, 158–159, 187, 197
Pertussis vaccine, 23
Pesticides, 12
  impact on children, 13
Pharmaceutical companies, and vaccination, 22
Pityrosporum ovale, cradle cap yeast, 63
Pizzorno, Lara, on spiritual training, 38–39
Polio vaccination, 25–26
Potentization, in homeopathy, 162
Prevention, in Oriental medicine, 138
Probiotics, 188–189
Protein powder, 193, 200

Provings, in homeopathy, 163
Psoriasis, 62, 63
Psyllium seed, 187–188
Pulsatilla (windflower), 178–180
Punishment, detrimental effects of, 33
Purified forms, 122

Q

Quercetin, 189–190
Quigley, Linda, 34

R

Recommended daily allowances (RDAs), 143, 147, 151b–152b
  for vegetarian children, 149, 150b
  for vitamin E, 193
Repertory, in homeopathy, 163
Rhus toxicodendron (poison ivy), 179
Rice Dream, 16
Ritalin (methylphenidate), 126, 127, 128, 134
Roos, Jackie, on spiritual training, 40–41
Rose hip tea, 17
Rosemary, 70, 102, 159, 197
Rubella (German measles) treatments for, 109–110
Ruta graveolens (rue), 179–180

S

Salk polio vaccine, 19
School lunch, health, 15
Scrimgeour, David, 137
Secretory IgA, 5, 6

Shaoyang syndrome, 65
Shiitake mushroom, 108, 111, 112
Shonishin (Japanese acupuncture), 139
Sinusitis, treatments for, 74–76
Skin care, 61–63
Sleep problems, treatments for,
    99–101
Sleeping with children, 33
Slippery elm, 88, 93, 103, 104, 188
Small pox vaccine, and HIV, 24
Smart Medicine for a Healthier Child,
    8
Snack list, 14b
Solter, Aletha, 31, 33
Sorbitol, in fruit juice, 16–17
Sore throat, treatments for, 92–93
Spirituality, training, 38–45
Spock, Benjamin, 14
St. John's wort (*Hypericum perforatum*),
    120, 123b, 174
Standarization, herbal compound,
    120, 123–124
Statistical-roulette approach, to
    health care, 24
Steffes, Sandra Apgar, 6
Stress hormones, in tears, 32
Styes, treatments for, 96–97
Sudden infant death syndrome (SIDS),
    and DPT, 26. *See also* Crib death
Sugar
  in fruit juice, 16, 17
  and immune function, 52
Sulfite detection, grape juice, 18
Sulphur, 180–181
Sunburn, treatments for, 101–102
Super Immunity for Kids, 191
Supplements. *See also* Food
    nutritional supplements, Mineral
    supplements, Nutritional supple-
    ments, Vitamin supplements
  for aches and pains, 71

for acne and pimples, 72
for anxiety and restlessness, 78
for asthma, 76–77
for athlete's foot, 79
for bedwetting, 99
for boils, 80
for burns, 81
for chickenpox, 107
for cold sores, 86–87
for colic, 68
for common cold, 85
for conjunctivitis, 96
for constipation, 103
for coughs, 88–89
for cuts, scrapes, and puncture
    wounds, 82
for diaper rash, 68–69
for diarrhea, 105
for earache, 95
for eczema, 73
for fever, 90
for fretfulness, 69
for gas, indigestion, and nausea, 106
for hay fever, 74
for head lice, 98
for influenza, 91
for insect bites and stings, 83
for insomnia, 101
for laryngitis, 93
for measles, 109
for mumps, 111–112
for rubella, 110
for sinusitis, 75–76
for sore throat, 93
for styes, 97
for sunburn, 102
for warts, 113
SV-40 monkey virus, 23
Swimming, and eczema and
    psoriasis, 63
Synthetics, and side effects, 118–119

T

T cell lymphocytes, 49
Tea
  diluted for fever rub, 56
  preparations, 122, 183
Tea tree oil, 71, 79, 81, 90, 160, 197
Tea Tree Oil Solution, 97
Teething, treatments for, 69–70
Tetanus vaccine, 27
Thermometers, 58
Thuja occidentalis, immune enhancer, 57
Thyme linalol, 89, 90, 161, 197
Tinctures, 120, 122, 182–183
Too Much Exercise Massage Oil, 70
"Toxicity index," CU study, 13
Trust, and crying, 32
Tui Na (Chinese massage therapy), 139
Tumeric, anti-inflammatory, 121
Tummy Ache Massage Formula, 105
Tylenol (acetaminophen), 56

U

UCLA Extension Lactation Training Program, 6
Ullman, Dana, 125
Ullman, Judyth Reichenberg, 126, 128
Ullman, Robert, 126
United Plant Savers (UPS), 124
University of California, Davis, 5
Usnea moss, 80

V

Vaccinations
  choosing, 29
  and crib death, 24
  injuries, 20
  medical exemption form, 30
  and pharmaceutical industry, 22
  reactions to, 19
Vaccination, Social Violence, and Criminality, 20
Vaccine failure, 22
Vegetarianism, for children, 149
Veratrum album, 127
Viral-related Diarrhea Massage Oil formula, 104
Virus season, natural remedy during, 51
Visualization, while breast-feeding, 5
Vitamin B, 193
Vitamin C
  and echinacea prior to starting school, 50
  and infantile scurvy, 150
  and juice for fever, 56
Vitamin deficiency, 118
  recognizing, 150, 152
Vitamin E, 192–193, 200
Vitamins, 144
  RDAs for children, 151b
Vitamin supplements, 190, 192–193
  home health kit, 200

W

Walnut flower essence, 131
Warts treatments for, 113
Weight-loss, while breast-feeding, 8
Weleda, soaps and shampoos, 61
Wenner, Paul, 12
What to Expect the First Year, 4
White grape juice, 17, 18
White willow, for fever, 56

Williams, Kathi, 19, 26, 29
Winter, Ruth, 61
Womanly Art of Breast-feeding, The, 3

X-Y

Xiao Chai Hu Tang, 65
Yeast overgrowth, and sugar, 17
Yogurt, for diaper rash, 62

Z

Zand, Janet, 8, 17
   preventing colds and flu, 53b
   on spiritual training, 39–40, 50
Zinc deficiency, in premature/low
    birth weight babies, 148–149
Zinc lozenges, 190